A Treasury of Asian Stories & Activities for Schools & Libraries

Cathy Spagnoli

Illustrations by
Paramasivam &
Michi Ukawa

Alleyside Press
Fort Atkinson, Wisconsin

Published by Alleyside Press, an imprint of Highsmith Press
Highsmith Press
W5527 Highway 106
P.O. Box 800
Fort Atkinson, Wisconsin 53538-0800
1-800-558-2110
hpress@highsmith.com
www.hpress.highsmith.com

© Cathy Spagnoli, 1998
Cover design: Frank Neu

The paper used in this publication meets the minimum requirements of American National Standard for Information Science — Permanence of Paper for Printed Library Material. ANSI/NISO Z39.48-1992.

Library of Congress Cataloging-in-Publication Data
   Spagnoli, Cathy.
      A treasury of Asian stories & activities for schools & libraries /
   Cathy Spagnoli ; illustrations by Paramasivam & Michi Ukawa.
        p. cm.
   Includes bibliographical references.
   ISBN 1-57950-006-4 (pbk. : alk. paper)
    1. Asian--Study and teaching (Primary)--Activities programs--United States. 2. Asia--Library resources. 3. Tales--Asia. I. Paramasivam. II. Ukawa, Michi. III. Title.
IN PROCESS
398.2æ095--dc21   98-15590
                                                                            CIP

Contents

For Gene & Harriet Spagnoli
who gave me a world rich
in stories and love

To Paramasivam & Manu
who enrich my world
every day

"Greetings" in Tamil language,
South Indian

Preface

In my search for stories, I have taught poetry to Tibetan dancers, trekked in Nepal, stayed in a Thai Buddhist monastery, and traveled throughout Korea, India, and Japan meeting hundreds of storytellers. In my home state of Washington, I have met many Southeast Asian refugees and immigrants who have graciously shared their tales with me.

From this work come many tales. Tales which give a glimpse of Asia, an Asia of tradition and change. It is an important time to learn from this region, home to more than half of the world's population and nine of the world's fifteen largest cities. And what better way to explore Asia than from the age-old yet contemporary art of the storyteller? For Asia remains one of the world's richest sources of varied storytelling materials and techniques.

The Asian tales here, for young listeners from preschool to third grade, come from South, Southeast, and East Asia. Across this large area there are countless differences in language, religion, dress, food, politics, and values which, although beyond the scope of this book, should be examined and remembered. At the same tim, there is also a growing sense of Asian pride and identity in the region, fueled by increased collaboration, as well as cultural and economic developments.

These simple tales, still shared in this dynamic region, are written to be told or read aloud. They can be learned easily by people with busy days or by student storytellers. Since people of various storytelling backgrounds may use this book, I begin with a few storytelling basics and then set the mood for Asian stories with several ideas from Asian storytelling. The next section features twenty stories selected for young listeners.

The themes of the tales reflect values and themes found in various Asian stories and cultures. The importance of friendship, wisdom, and humor shines through, along with the need to be kind and to cooperate. The stories remind listeners to use their wits, to work hard, to respect parents, while they warn against greed and pride. And since most cultures, everywhere, have their heroes and ghosts, those are found here as well.

A proverb from the country is included before each story as another little piece of that land. Because young listeners love to sing, to make and do, I've also added an educational activity from the culture to complement every story. Another element is a library/information skills activity related to either the story or the educational activity kindly added by Don Sager.

Each story unit concludes with additional suggestions for books to share. Since the number of books on each country varies so greatly, I limited myself to picture books related to the story or activity, and to some exceptionally recommended titles from major bibliographies of multicultural children's books. Asian words sounds and names are used liberally throughout. Pronunciation hints are included when possible, but the best help is always a native speaker. You'll find Asian names written family name first if that is the case in the native language.

In addition to original art by Michi Ukawa and Paramasivam, design and textile patterns reflecting the unique artistic traditions of these countries have been added.

Finally, you'll find a resource list with books, Internet sites, and centers/stores stocking Asian materials you can order for your programs. Brief notes on story sources then end the book.

Acknowledgments

I wish to thank the World Music Press, the Seattle Children's Museum, and Cliff Sloane, who have so kindly allowed me to use their printed material. And I am grateful to Nancy Knies and Don Sager of Highsmith Press for their enthusiasm, talent and trust.

Many people have helped me to learn about Asian storytelling over the years. To them goes all the credit for this book, while I am solely to blame for any mistakes. In the story notes, I have included the gracious people who told me their tales and songs. There are many other names which should be listed here, including my wonderful family, and the tellers who shared so much with me, but space limits me to the following groups which helped especially as I gathered material for this book:

The Korea Foundation and The Korea Society,

The Japan Foundation,

Chinese Information and Service Center (Seattle),

Refugee Women's Alliance (Seattle),

Vashon Library and King County Library System Interlibrary Loan Department,

Cholamandal Artists Village (India),

Banyan Teacher Centre (India),

Asian Outreach Centers at the University of Washington.

Storytelling Basics

Well begun is half done. **Korean proverb**

Emurisan, a traditional Japanese teller, was once asked when he told his first tale. He said that he listened and listened to his grandparents tell tales as he grew.One day at the age of ten, he sat at a family gathering, hearing more stories. Suddenly, his grandfather turned to him and said, "Now it is your turn."

And, now it is your turn to tell more Asian tales, and to introduce your listeners to Asian countries through words, images, melodies, and crafts.

The stories in this book were chosen for younger listeners, but they can be told by any age. In fact, these tales may be useful to student storytellers seeking material for young audiences. With these dual purposes in mind, the following suggestions are addressed both to beginning tellers and to adult guides of student storytellers.

Choosing a Story

Work on a story which appeals to you and which suits the interests and needs of your listeners. Look for tales that are good to tell, ones with:

- limited and clearly drawn characters,
- a plot that moves,
- pleasing language and sounds,
- vivid images,
- elements of humor, suspense, or drama,
- possibilities for actions and audience participation.

Learning the Tale

Visualize the story. Reread it several times, then try to picture it scene by scene. Go back to the original occasionally to see how you've changed the story. Find the version you're comfortable with, make sure that it seems the right length—without any rambling, yet with enough material to satisfy your listeners. Tell it to yourself, a friend, the tape recorder. Repeat it until you feel comfortable.

Polishing It

When you know the basic story well, play with it and bring it fully to life. Add gestures that capture a character or an action. Use language that paints pictures, with details that pull your listeners into the tale. Try a pause or perhaps some repetition. Experiment with sounds from the setting, or a character's voice. Consider ideas for audience participation. If you wish to try a prop, see the next section for descriptions of a few Asian props.

As the polished story develops, edit out all "uhs," "ums," as well as any nervous mannerisms which could distract. A tape recorder will help you to catch hesitations, unnecessary repetitions, and weak images as you also double check the length, rhythm, and timing of your telling.

Using Feedback

To tell a story in front of a group is difficult for many people. Allow for enough time and preparation, be easy on yourself. If you are helping students, encourage their efforts and try to find their storytelling strengths: some students will have a flair for humor or the dramatic, others may use language particularly well, some will make excellent props.

As you practice, use the following list to gently critique yourself. When working with students, have them practice in pairs and small groups. Provide them with a copy of the following checklist.

✔ Do the words give details and create images?

✔ Are actions and facial expressions used effectively?

✔ Are nervous gestures distracting?

✔ Is the voice expressive, clear, and loud enough?

✔ If character voices are tried, are they consistent and effective?

✔ Are sound effects used well?

✔ Could a pause be added to build suspense or underline an image?

✔ Is the teller sensitive to the audience?

✔ If props are used, do they add to story or distract?

✔ If audience participation is encouraged, is it working?

✔ If the story too long, too short, or just right?

Performing

Once the story is ready, it needs to be told and retold. Try it in front of different audiences, too, and notice how the story changes in response to their reactions. Find every chance you can to tell your stories and remind students of all the places to share a tale: babysitting, at the dinner table, on trips, camping, in scouts, at parties, on the playground, at bedtime.

Before you tell, remember to relax: take a good breath, yawn, stretch. Then enjoy. You are giving a gift to your listeners, one which enriches all of you.

Adding an Asian Touch

Stories can be used in several ways to introduce parts of Asia to listeners. Sometimes, tales are shared because they are similar to stories young children in the U.S. already know, such as the many Asian versions of *Cinderella*. At other times, a particular tale can be used as part of a multicultural exploration of a theme: friendship, nature, family. Or if time and interest allow, several stories can be used for an in-depth focus on Asia.

Preparing the Environment

To use any approach well, it is helpful if the class, library, or home environment encourages children to explore the cultural settings of the tales. A small collection of books about various Asian countries can be put out and a bulletin board can display photos to pull children into another land.

Various articles can also share cultural roots: household tools, toys, clothing and textiles, posters, pictures, maps, music tapes and instruments, flags, spices for cooking, food snacks. Such items can often be borrowed from community members, museum education departments, libraries, regional Asian outreach centers at universities, or located through the resource section in the back of the book.

Once you've done what you can with the setting, try adding some of the these Asian tools to your telling…

Language and Sound

A Japanese dog doesn't bark "bow-wow," he goes "wan, wan." A Korean frog croaks, "kae-gul, kae-gul," not "ribbet, ribbet." Sounds and images from different Asian languages can be sprinkled in for wonderful effects when you tell. Start a file of Asian words, images, and sound effects to use in your tales. Here are a few sounds to try from the rich possibilities of Japanese onomatopoeia.

Japanese Sound	Pronunciation	Meaning
chira chira	chee-rah	a weak light flickering
choko choko	choh-koh	to toddle
datt datt	daht	engine sound
doshin	doh-shin	something heavy falling
gacha gacha	gah-chah	rattle, clatter
kan kan	kahn	blazing sunshine; anger
kari kari	kah-ree	being nervous, excited
niko niko	nee-koh	to smile warmly
pachi pachi	pah-chee	blinking, crackling
potari	poh-tah-ree	a dripping sound

Music

In many Asian storytelling traditions, music and instruments are very important. Long ballads tell involved stories, and many storytelling styles have a vibrant blend of speech and song.

Percussive and stringed instruments are most popular: bells, drums, lutes, fiddles, clay pots, a musical bow in South India. Even the Chinese *hsing-mu*, a simple block of wood, can effectively represent sounds found in a tale: thunder, footsteps, a fight, and a sad farewell.

In many Asian styles, a musician accompanies the teller, adding interest and drama to the story. Such collaboration is great for student tellers to attempt, and a tape recorder can help them see if the balance of music and words is about right.

To add a musical touch, locate different Asian instruments, tapes, and song materials in the resource section or use the songs from this book. Then, whether working alone or with others, try using music to:

- show a character with a musical theme;
- create mood through a sound texture, rhythm, melody;
- reinforce an image by a single sound;
- give musical sound effects;
- portray movement in plot through rhythmic change;
- introduce beginning/ending through certain music.

Costume

Some tales are told in costume in Asia, although for young and beginning tellers, a hint of a costume might be the best answer. A clever storyteller can learn from the many uses of the Cambodian *krama*, a long cotton or silk scarf. It can be:

- wrapped around the forehead and tied in back, to keep off sweat;
- twisted into a rope, then shaped in a circle and put on the head under a heavy object to help carry it;
- draped diagonally across a woman's chest and tied at shoulder or waist;
- worn like a cloth belt over a shirt;
- hung as a baby's hammock on trees;
- wrapped around the body for bathing;
- shaped into a cloth doll or ball and played with.

Props

Across Asia, many wonderful storytelling props are used. They provide not only a way to capture attention, but also an opportunity to share visual details of a culture, past and present. A Japanese storytelling friend, while sharing *Momotaro (Peach Boy)* with Japanese children, once said, "The old woman did her washing by the stream." When she asked children to draw pictures from the tale afterwards, several drawings featured a modern washing machine next to a stream. "From that moment," she said, "I decided to use more *kamishibai* (story cards) of old tales, so that children can see how it used to be."

Below are brief descriptions of several props from Asia; another suggestion or two will be found later with the stories. These ideas can, with imagination and ingenuity, be easily adapted for your telling, or by students. Most of the scrolls mentioned below, for example, can be re-created quite well on large roll paper, with either markers or construction paper cut-outs.

Patas

These vertical scrolls are used in North India. They're each about one foot wide and up to twenty feet long, with large rectangular panels showing scenes from the story. Stories vary from older tales of various gods to newer court cases of accidents and crime, tales of the Indian freedom fight, or stories about the dowry system and family planning. The tales are told by wandering tellers who unroll the scrolls slowly as they tell.

Phad

This is a long (to fifteen feet x four feet high), brightly painted storytelling scroll found in Rajasthan state, North India. These horizontal scrolls often show large drawings of main characters in the center, with various smaller images from the story scattered around them. The phad is set up on bamboo poles, usually outdoors, and the performance often lasts all night. The teller sings, dances, and plays a many stringed fiddle during the story narration. His wife accompanies him with song and illuminates the relevant story scenes with a lantern. Members of the audience join in on familiar refrains and follow the story eagerly. The most commonly told story is that of Pabuji, a fourteenth century regional hero.

Kalamkari

Large kalamkari temple hangings are sometimes used for storytelling in South India. The painted cloth is made by an involved process using natural dyes, buffalo milk, and running stream water to set the dyes. The composition of the cloths vary—sometimes an entire story is shown in a linear sequence of small boxes, sometimes just one important scene is illustrated, with big characters. A line of text is at times written above the pictures, providing a small piece of the story. The teller sits in front of the cloth, using it as a backdrop as he narrates the tales of the gods pictured on the cloth.

Kamishibai

Years ago, the Japanese kamishibai teller carried colorful hand-painted sets of large story cards as he cycled around. Each twelve to sixteen card set visually related, in sequence, either an entire tale or part of one—serials were popular and stretched on for countless months. The teller gathered a crowd, sold candy and rice snacks to the audience, then showed the cards in a small wooden stage mounted on the back of his bike. With expression and energy, he told varied tales: samurai stories, Chinese legends, science fiction, comic tales, even the "Lone Ranger." Today, both lovely handmade sets and printed cards are used in libraries and schools, but the traveling tellers are very rare.

Fan

A folding fan—both closed and fully or partially opened—is a part of story-telling in both Japanese *rakugo* and Korean *p`ansori* telling. In the theatri-cal singing style of p'ansori, it is used for emphasis and dramatic effect. In the hands of a skilled rakugo teller, it can portray a sword, *shamisen* (lute), pipe, pole, pot, writing brush, bowl, screen, and more.

An Asian Storytelling Setting

Invite your audience to a storytelling event with pretty paper programs. Paper arts in Asia are very popular: Chinese papercuts, woodblock prints in Nepal and East Asia, Japanese origami, and handmade paper from flow-ers and plants in much of Asia. Make your own adaptations; if you are lucky enough to know someone who writes an Asian language, include a bit of the script to add interest.

Display cultural objects, have visuals (including calligraphy) on the wall, and, if possible, tapes of music playing as the audience enters. Even the floor can be decorated, perhaps with the beautiful designs called *kolams* in South India. They often include important cultural symbols: a temple cart, lotus, peacock, oil lamp, or the signs of a certain deity, but are made also simply in pleasing geometrical shapes. (See "Kachba," p. 21–22, for a few samples.) Find or create similar arts of temporary beauty to use in your setting.

If possible, seat your audience on the floor, as is done in most of Asia. Have lighting which is relaxed, although today everything from bright flu-orescent lights to lovely oil lamps illuminate storytelling events in the diverse countries of Asia.

Storytelling festivals in some Asian lands have tea shops and food stalls set up temporarily to help keep listeners awake through long sessions. Offering a snack or drink from Asia would be great fun when you share these tales.

And finally, when your audience leaves, you might consider an *omiyage*, a souvenir, as they say in Japan. Hospitality is very important in most Asian cultures and gift giving can be a part of that. Any small memento would be lovely for your listeners:

- a simple craft or folk toy,
- calligraphy,
- a snack to eat,
- origami,
- bookmark,
- a poem, riddle, or proverb from the culture, or
- a story written down to be told again and again and again...

Chapter 1

Japan

The tongue is more to be feared than the sword.

Japan has become a major economic power in the Pacific Rim while keeping alive a rich cultural heritage. Storytelling traditions in Japan include the wandering teller with *biwa* (lute) of old, as well as today's sophisticated art of *rakugo* and the warm telling in friendly *bunko*, home libraries which cater to neighborhood children. The use of onomatopoeia is especially noteworthy in Japanese telling, as are the many marvelous creatures which move through Japanese folklore.

The Two Tengu

Mukashi, mukashi...
Long ago in Japan, people told tales of *tengu*.
Tengu had **big** noses in front and small wings in back.
They were tricky, and sometimes a little bit bad.

Now in those older days, two tengu were neighbors.
One was very red, the other was very blue.
And they were best friends.
They ran together, *to-ko, to-ko.*
They flew together, *su-ii, su-iiii.*
But they fought together, too. They fought about rice.

"My rice is nicer than yours," said the red tengu.
"No, **mine** is," declared the blue. They fought about clothes.

"My belt is better than yours," said the red tengu.
"No, **mine** is," said the blue. Yet one day they grew bored fighting about the same old things.
So they sat sighing, trying to find something new to do.
They scratched their heads. They scratched their ears.
They scratched their long noses.

"I know! Let's have a nose contest!" cried the blue tengu.
"My nose is the very best nose. It grows so long.
It can go far, far away. Just wait and see!"

He sat down on a hill. He pointed his nose down.
Then he stretched and stretched and stretched it. *Suuuuuuuuuiiiiiiiiii*
It flew through the breeze.
It flew over trees.
It flew to a large castle and into the room of a princess.

Pronunciation notes for tale and activity:
"a" as ah
"e" as in egg
"g" is hard g
"i" as ee
"o" as oh
"oi" as in boy
"u" as oo

"Look," she cried. "A blue pole! How lovely.
Just what I need to hold my new clothes."
Happily, she draped all of her lovely kimonos on the pole.

Far away, the blue tengu sat still on the hill, until his nose felt just too itchy.
He pulled it quickly back. As it flew, most of the kimonos fell off.
They floated down like bright kites.

But the last one dropped right next to the blue tengu.
With a grin, he tried it on.
It was shiny and new, a perfect fit, too.

"Thank you, nose!" he said. Then he ran to his friend and bragged,
"My nose went far away. And it brought me a gift."

"My nose is better," said the red tengu. "Just see what I get."
He sat down on the hill.
He stretched and stretched and stretched his nose. *Suuuuuuuuuiiiiiii*
It flew through the breeze, over trees, and right to that big castle.
But not to the same room.
The red nose went next door to the room of the prince.
And he was learning karate.

"Look!" he cried to his teacher.
"A snake. A big red snake! It might bite us."

So the prince hit the poor nose, ***do-shi! do-shi!***
Far away on the hill, the red tengu cried in pain.
He pulled his nose quickly back.
But now the nose was red and black and blue.
He started to sob, *na-ku, na-ku.*

When the blue tengu heard his friend crying, he ran to him.
He saw the sore nose and felt very, very sad.
"I'm so sorry that your nose hurts," he said.
"You are my best friend. I want you happy.
Let's stop this nose contest. Let's stop all of our fights."

"That sounds good," said the red tengu,
rubbing his poor nose.
So the two beat their nicest drums
and sang their favorite songs.
They celebrated their new peace.
After that, they fought much less.
And they laughed much more.
So the two tengu lived happily ever after
as best, best, best friends.

For Further Exploration of Japan

Japan, also known as Nippon (origin of the sun); East Asia
Area: 145,826 sq. miles
Population: 125,449,703 (1996 est.); 78% urban
Official language: Japanese
Largest city: Tokyo (8,019,938 1995 est.)

Activity: Wordplay

Just as onomatopoeia adds interest to this little tale, wordplay games add cross-cultural fun to your setting. Here are two to try.

Naka, naka, hoi!

This one can be sung, but young children find it easier to chant the three words while doing one specific action, described below, for each word.

naka (in) *tap lap with both hands*
soto (out) *move hands out slightly to sides*
hoi (Oh!) *hands push out in front of chest*

Repeat words and actions faster and faster. Younger children can try just the first three lines. Older children can attempt the whole song.

Naka, naka, hoi! Soto, soto, hoi!
Naka, soto, soto, naka,
Naka, naka, hoi!

Soto, soto, hoi! Soto, soto, hoi!
Soto, naka, naka, soto,
Soto, soto, hoi!

Word Chains

Japanese children enjoy making chains linked by repetitions of words or syllables. In the example below, the chain starts in the second line with the word "square" and continues when "square" is repeated as the first word in the third line, and so on. Try this chain, then use the formula to have children make their own.

Sa-yo-na-ra san-ka-ku	Farewell to triangle
Ma-ta ki-te shi-ka-ku	Come again square
Shi-ka-ku wa to-fu	Square is tofu
To-fu wa shi-roi	Tofu is white
Shi-roi wa u-sa-gi.	White is a rabbit.

Library/Information Skills Activity

If your library has an electronic multimedia encyclopedia, this would be a good opportunity to have children conduct a general search. Ask them to look up Japan. Have students write down three things they thought were interesting in the information they found. This same activity can be used with print encyclopedias.

Books to Share

For more on Japanese creatures, try these three picture books:

Spagnoli, Cathy. *Oni Wa Soto*. Bothell: The Wright Group, 1995.

Matsutani, Miyoko. *The Witch's Magic Cloth*. New York: Lothrop, Lee & Shepard, 1983.

Another good book for children ages five to seven is:

Stamm, Claus. *Three Strong Women: A Tall Tale from Japan*. New York: Viking, 1990. An age-old Japanese tale in which the main character is "Forever Mountain."

Chapter 2

Burma

What starts small can grow big,
What quickly grows big can grow small too.

In Burma today, a long battle is going on for freedom and independence. Aung San Suu Kyi, a brave woman and daughter of one of Burma's early heroes, leads the movement for a free and democratic country. While the struggle continues, though, people go on about their lives, following the teachings of the Buddha, and sharing stories such as these which encourage traditional values of simplicity and cooperation.

The Kind Crow

Once upon a time in Burma, a young girl lived with her poor mother. The two had very little to eat but shared a rich love. Every day they went to work in the fields. Every night they ate a little rice then went to bed.

One morning the girl sat outside, guarding the rice grains they had just picked. Many birds circled round, eager to eat, but the girl kept them all away. Not one grain was taken until, all of a sudden, a crow swooped down.

With a loud *caw,* he landed on the rice. His head moved up and down, up and down as he picked and pecked the grains. The girl waved her arms and shouted at him, but he didn't stop. Finally, the girl began to cry.

"Oh my poor mother," she sobbed. "What will she say? We need this rice. Now we will starve." The crow felt suddenly sad. He turned to her and said, "I will pay for this. Come tonight to the big tamarind tree." Then off he flew.

That evening, while her mother rested, the girl quietly crept to the tree. She looked up and was amazed to see a little house made of shining gold. As she stood staring, the crow looked out.

"Ah, you've come. I'll let down a ladder," he said. "Would you like one of gold, silver, or brass?"

"Oh, a simple brass one is fine," replied the girl. But a lovely gold ladder came down instead. Up, up, up the girl climbed, then she squeezed into the house.

"You must be hungry," said the crow. "Will you eat on a dish of gold, silver, or brass?"

"Plain brass is good enough for me," said the girl. But she was served a delicious meal on a dish of purest gold.

"You have been very nice and you are not greedy," said the crow. "I wish to give you something to take home. Would you like a big box, a medium box, or a small one?"

"Well, you didn't really eat that much rice," said the girl fairly. "So I'll just take the smallest one." The crow gave her the little box and the girl climbed happily down, after thanking him again and again.

She ran back to her mother and they opened the box. Inside were precious rubies and gems. They cried with joy then ran to share their good fortune with friends all round.

But in the same village lived a greedy girl and her greedier mother. When they heard the story of the kind crow, they wanted money as well. So one day, the girl sat outside with some rice grains.

Birds flew down and she let them all eat while she dozed. By the time the crow came, there was little left. But as soon as he ate three grains, she cried crossly, "Now you have to pay for all the rice since you took so long, silly bird. Give me some gold from your tree house."

"Please come this evening then," said the crow politely as he left. The girl could hardly wait for the sun to set. Finally at dusk she raced to the tree, shouting, "Hurry and let me in."

"Would you like a ladder of gold, silver, or brass?" asked the crow.

"The gold one, of course," yelled the girl. But a brass one came down. She climbed up and pushed her way into the house.

"Feed me something quick," she ordered.

"Would you like to eat on gold, silver, or brass?"

"On gold and right away," she demanded. But only a bit of hard rice was served slowly on a brass plate.

"Well, this is boring," she said. "I'm going. And you owe me a box."

"Would you like a big box, a medium one, or a small one?" asked the crow sweetly.

"I'm not a fool," she snapped. "I'll take the biggest, of course." So the crow held out a large box. She snatched it and left without even a thank you. Back to her house she stumbled, lugging the heavy box and dreaming of riches inside. Her mother eagerly joined her and the two tore the box open.

Yet inside, as you can guess, they didn't find any treasure. Instead, a horrible, huge snake came out, hissed loudly, licked their skin, and scared them terribly. Then, luckily for that greedy pair, he decided not to bite. With a final *sssssss*, he slithered away. And maybe then the two were a little nicer, a little less greedy. But maybe not.

For Further Exploration of Burma

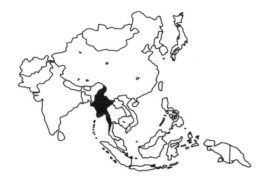

Burma, officially known as the Union of Myanmar;
  Southeast Asia
Area: 261,218 sq. miles
Population: 45,975,625; 75 percent rural
Official language: Burmese
Largest city: Yangon (formerly known as Rangoon)

Activity: Game of Three Squares

This little Burmese game of tag echoes the theme of three in the story. Three large squares are drawn with chalk or made with sticks or stones on the ground, in three places. Children in a row are counted out by the first rhyme until only two are left. Then the second rhyme is said and the child left is *It*. All children then quickly run off while *It* tries to catch them. Whenever they stand in a house, they are safe. After several children are caught, the game starts again with the rhymes and a new *It*.

The palm sugar in the rhyme is a hard, dark sugar made from the sugar palm trees of South and Southeast Asia. The tree is much admired not only for the sugar, juice, and alcohol it provides, but also for the timber and craft items produced from its trunk.

Made of lines
Three houses
Just for us
Off you go
Save yourself and run.

Palm juice
Palm sugar
Palm sugar lumps
Bend over, take some.
Now, follow me.

Library/Information Skills Activity

Stories and folk tales from around the world have also proven more about how people and places are alike than different because the lessons they teach are often the same. Discuss fables and folk tales with students. Identify where these kinds of stories can be found in the library.

If there is time have students talk about other stories they might know where greed is punished or where honesty and effort are rewarded, e.g., "Jack and the Bean Stalk," "Cinderella."

Books to Share

There are still too few picture books about Burma, but the following are recommended.

Froese, Deborah. *The Wise Washerman.* New York: Hyperion Books, 1996. A recent folktale with good illustrations.

Aung, San Suu Kyi. *Burma (Myanmar).* Broomall, PA: Chelsea House, 1988. A nonfiction book for older children from the "Let's Visit Places & Peoples of the World Series."

Wright, David. *Burma.* Chicago: Children's Press, 1991. Another nonfiction look at Burma.

Chapter 3

Cambodia

Even the big ships need the little boats to guide them to shore.

Cambodia is a lovely land that has suffered much in the last decades. Too many in Cambodia were killed during the recent war; too many were made homeless and turned into refugees. But the solace of Buddhism and the strength and humor of the Cambodians have helped those who came to the U.S. Some brought with them stories of a favorite Cambodian trickster, Judge Rabbit. Judge Rabbit tricks other animals, as in this tale, but he also helps humans and animals to find justice, even when a human judge cannot.

Judge Rabbit & Tiger

Tiger was mad.
Judge Rabbit had tricked him again.
Poor Tiger's tail hurt because of that trick.
So he was chasing Rabbit to teach him a lesson.

"I'll get you, Rabbit," he roared, running through the forest. Rabbit ran and ran and ran, too, as quickly as he could. But he heard Tiger close behind.

"Tiger runs fast," thought Judge Rabbit. "So I'll have to think even faster."

Just then Rabbit saw a bee's nest on a tree. He climbed quickly up and sat next to it. Carefully he took a leaf, licked it, and put it over the door hole.

Angry bees were suddenly trapped inside the nest. They wanted to get out. They buzzed and buzzed very, very loudly. And the buzzing sounded like a special kind of drum.

Judge Rabbit pulled back his arm, then swung it almost to the nest. He pretended to hit the nest, but of course he was most careful not to. Back and forth his arm waved, as if beating a fine steady sound on a drum. Tiger came up and stood under the tree.

"I've got you now, Rabbit," he growled. "And I'm going to eat you up."

"Not now, Tiger," cried Judge Rabbit. "Later you can eat me. Right now I'm too busy."

"Busy doing what?" asked Tiger as he watched Rabbit, who seemed to be hitting something.

"I'm playing the drum for the angels above," he replied. "They love this music so they'll give me grand gifts."

Tiger listened. *Bzzzz. Bzzzz. Bzzzz.* It did sound quite nice, like a finely tuned drum. He didn't think about bees. He didn't recognize the bee's nest. He just thought about all the gifts Rabbit was getting. So Tiger felt jealous.

"Rabbit, I want to play the drum and get gifts," he said.

"Sorry, Tiger," said Rabbit. "It's my turn."

"Please, Rabbit," pleaded Tiger. "Please let me play."

"But if you come up here, you'll eat me," Rabbit replied.

"No, no, I promise I won't," said Tiger. "Let me play and I'll be your friend forever."

"*Welllll,*" said Rabbit.

"*Pleeeeeease,*" begged Tiger.

"Oh, all right," said Rabbit. "I'll go find another drum. You climb up here and watch me. When I jump up and down three times, hit that drum as hard as you can. The angels will love it!"

"*Akoon, akoon,*" said Tiger, thanking Judge Rabbit again and again. Then Rabbit came down and started to run.

akoon: thanks

Tiger climbed up slowly and sat next to the drum. He watched and waited for Rabbit's signal. At last he saw the three big jumps. With a grin, he took his hand and gave the drum *one huge hit.*

Bzzzzzzzzzzz *Bzzzzzzzzzzz* **Bzzzzzzzzzzz**

The nest broke. Hundreds of furious bees raced out. Tiger jumped down and tried to run but the bees followed right behind. Those angry bees chased him for a long, long time.

As for Rabbit, he was far, far away, and quite safe. He wiggled his ears, munched his favorite cucumbers, and thought about poor Tiger, tricked again.

A type of tiger used in Asian tapestries.

For Further Exploration of Cambodia

Cambodia, also known as Kampuchea; Southeast Asia
Area: 69,898 sq. miles
Population: 10,861,218 (1996 est.); 85 % rural
Official language: Khmer (Cambodian)
Largest city: Phnom Penh

Activity: Leak Kanseng (Hide the Scarf)

Judge Rabbit is not the only trickster in Cambodia. A clever boy, usually called A chey, plays tricks of all kinds, first against his master, then the king, and even the Chinese emperor. Urge children to be a bit tricky, too, as they play and enjoy Leak Kanseng.

A rectangular scarf is tied into a bundle and children sit in a circle to play this popular game remembered by musician Sam-ang Sam. One child, *It*, walks around the outside of the circle, with the scarf.

Children sing a song whose words means:

> *Hide the scarf.*
> *The cat is biting my heel,*
> *and drags my leg.*

As they sing, *It* quietly drops the scarf behind a seated child's back. When she notices the scarf, she picks it up and chases *It*. If *It* makes it back to the vacant spot in circle, then the chaser is now *It* and the game continues. If not, the old *It* can try again!

Leak Kanseng
Hide the Scarf

Leak kan seng chhma khaim keng oh long oh long.

Library/Information Skills Activity

The World Wide Web (WWW) offers a rich variety of valuable information to even young students. If your library or school offers student access to the web, use this as an opportunity to show the students a hierarchical search using the just-for-kids search engine in Yahoo <http://www.yahooligans.com>. From this home page select Around the World and then Countries. Here you'll find current as well background information on many of the countries of Asia. Select Cambodia and you can choose to look at the Cambodian Embassy site or look at a map of the country.

Books to Share

Here are some more Judge Rabbit tales:

Spagnoli, Cathy and Lina Mao Wall. *Judge Rabbit Meets the Tree Spirit.* San Francisco: Children's Book Press, 1991.

Spagnoli, Cathy. *Judge Rabbit Helps the Fish.* Bothell, WA: The Wright Group, 1995.

Ho, Minfong. *Brother Rabbit.* New York: Lothrop, Lee & Shepard, 1997.

Another good book for older children:

Ho, Minfong. *The Clay Marble.* New York: Farrar, Straus and Giroux, 1991. This relates the story of a young girl and her family who flee the horrors of the Cambodian War to find safety.

Chapter 4

Bangladesh

One son means a bed of flowers,
Five sons mean a bed of thorns.

Bangladesh, although small in size, has a rich tradition of literature and art. When the British colonialists left in 1947, it was called East Pakistan. But while linked by Islam with West Pakistan, its cultural roots are quite different, thus it fought for and achieved independence in 1971. An agricultural country with a large population, it suffers often from flooding. But its stories and culture remain treasures to share.

The Rich Sparrow

One day, a sparrow found a small coin in the forest.
Overjoyed, she returned to her nest, singing over and over,
"I'm as rich as the king,
I'm as rich as the king."

The next day the king was riding through the woods,
when he suddenly heard the song.
"What a silly sparrow," he growled. "She can't be as rich as I am."

But the sparrow just kept chirping,
"I'm as rich as the king,
I'm as rich as the king."

The king grew more and more annoyed.
Finally he called to his guards, "Go bring me that silly bird."
Guards scurried up the tree, but found only a nest.
And in the nest, one tiny coin. They brought it to the king.
He looked at it and laughed; it was so small.

But just then he heard the sparrow sing,
"The king's a thief, he stole my coin,
The king's a thief, he stole my coin."

"Catch that worthless sparrow," roared the king.
Dashing here and there, his men chased after the sparrow.
They threw sticks and stones as branches fell all over them.
They knocked into each other, but they didn't get the bird.
While they raced round and round, the sparrow sang out,
"The king's men can't catch me,
The king's men can't catch me."

Furious now, the king sent for the royal hunters.
After several tries, they trapped the sparrow.
They carried her to the palace while she chirped,
"The king's home will be my home,
The king's home will be my home."

In the palace, the king told the cook,
"Fry her right away. I shall eat her for dinner."
But when the cook reached for the sparrow, she suddenly flew off.
Much upset, the cook fried a frog instead and covered it with a
delicious, rich sauce. At dinner, the king ate his food, well satisfied.

"That awful sparrow is gone at last," he said with a burp.
Yet just then, the sparrow flew in, singing,
"The foolish king just ate a frog,
The foolish king just ate a frog."

The king felt suddenly ill. He threw a royal sandal at the sparrow.
But it hit a fine old painting instead, which dropped to the floor, ruined.
So the sparrow sang,
"The silly king can't hit me,
The silly king can't hit me."

"Catch that sparrow!" roared the king, jumping in rage.
At last the sparrow was caught, once again.
"Now," said the king. "I shall swallow it whole."
He called for some water to help push it down.
And he asked two big soldiers, with fine large swords,
to stand on either side of him.

"If this sparrow somehow escapes,
use your swords and slice it in two!" he told them.
Eagerly, the king shoved the sparrow into his mouth,
just as his young daughter came in singing sweetly.
The king laughed happily when he heard her voice.

Yet when he opened his mouth, the sparrow flew out.
At once, two sharp swords cut through the air.
But they missed the sparrow.
Instead, they neatly sliced off the tip of the king's large royal nose.
And the sparrow flew swiftly away, singing,
"The rich bird sings, but your nose stings.
(softer and slower to end story)
The rich bird sings, but your nose stings."

• **Bangladesh** • *The Rich Sparrow*   17

For Further Exploration of Bangladesh

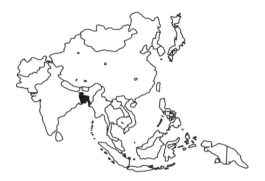

Bangladesh, officially known as the People's Republic of Bangladesh; South Asia
Area: 55,598 sq. miles
Population: 109,876,977 (1991 est.); 80% rural
Official language: Bangla
Largest city: Dhaka

Activity: Rhymes

Here are two fine rhymes chanted widely by children in Bangladesh and kindly shared by Hasnain Sabih and his son Nayak.

The first poem plays with rhymes, rhythms, and nonsense words to paint a humorous picture of a devoted son-in-law in a society that values family greatly.

The *kantha* (quilt) of the second rhyme is an important folk art in Bangladesh. It is made from layers of old cloth joined together by a running stitch. Especially beautiful ones are made from white saris covered with finely embroidered plants, figures, animals, and more.

Aikom Baikom Taratari

Aikom baikom taratari
Jodu Mashtar shoshur bari
Rail kompo jhomajhom
Jodu Mashtar alum dom.

Aikom baikom Jodu Master (teacher)
Runs for in-law's in a haste,
Rail journey full of jerking
Made Jodu like potato paste.

Sheet Amar Meet

Sheet amar meet
Agun amar bhai
Sheetere koiya dio
Kantha kapor nai.

Winter is my friend,
though my brother is fire.
Tell winter—we don't have
quilts, nor clothes to wear.

Pronunciation: "a" as ah, "ai" as I, except in rail, "i" as ee, "o" as oh, "or" as or, "oi" as in boy, "u" as oo.

Library/Information Skills Activity

Bangladesh is the eighth largest nation in the world in terms of population. This presents a good opportunity to introduce older children to a common reference book that provides current country information. Show the students how to use the Quick Thumb Index on the back of the *World Almanac*. Help them locate the Nations of the World tab and show them how this helps them go right to the country information in the book. Help students find Bangladesh. Then ask them to locate the capital city and determine its population.

For a more extensive unit, you'll find the address for the countries' embassies listed at the end of the entries. Embassies can be a rich source of free materials about their homelands.

Books to Share

Bailey, Donna and Anna Sproule. *Bangladesh (Where We Live)*. Chatham, NJ: Steck-Vaughn, 1991. A child living in Dhaka describes everyday life and celebrations in Bangladesh.

Bangladesh is largely Muslim, so try this book of rhymes which share Muslim culture.

McDermott, Mustafa Yusuf. *Muslim Nursery Rhymes*. Leicester, U.K.: Islamic Foundation, 1981.

Chapter 5

India

The girl who could not dance blamed the slope of the stage.

From the northern Himalayan mountains to Kerala's quiet backwaters in the south, India is a rich mosaic of languages, cultures, and stories. And not only are there thousands of stories, but also hundreds of different ways to tell them. Storytellers work alone, in partners, in groups, with music or without, with scrolls, hangings, costume. But tales are also told simply, as you can this tale from North India.

Kachba

Long ago in India dwelt a lively princess. As she grew older, her parents planned her wedding. For her husband they chose Kachba, a kind prince from a nearby kingdom. One day, while her parents talked of the future, the princess walked in the garden. All of a sudden, her maids began to giggle and tease her, chanting, *"You will marry Kachba, You will marry Kachba."*

Now the princess didn't yet know of the wedding plans. She didn't know that Kachba was a very nice prince. She only knew that *kachba* meant turtle in her language. So she was terribly upset.

"No, No, No! I'll never marry a turtle," she cried. But they kept on singing, *"You will marry Kachba, You will marry Kachba."*

"No, No!" she shouted. "I will **not** marry a silly old turtle."

And when they kept teasing, she ran into the palace and into her room. There she cried and cried and cried. At last her mother, the queen, came in and asked, "Why are you so upset, my dear?"

"My maids say I have to marry Kachba," sobbed the princess. "But I can't marry a turtle, mother, I just can't."

"Silly girl," said the mother. "Kachba is a young man and a wise prince, not a turtle. He is gentle and good; you will make a fine couple."

"But his name means turtle. Everyone will laugh at me," cried the princess.

"Not at all," said the queen. "Everyone will love Kachba for his kind heart."

But nothing the queen said helped her daughter. The princess continued to cry until the king came in. He stomped and shouted and ordered her to stop. But she kept right on crying, "I won't marry a turtle, I won't!"

"All right, all right," roared the king at last. "We'll stop the wedding. But you are being a fool. It's only a name." And he stormed out to send word to Kachba. A messenger rode and rode and finally bowed before Kachba and his father, the king.

"Please excuse me, kind sirs," he said with respect. "But I am afraid that our princess can not marry Kachba."

"Why not?" demanded the king. "We have planned the wedding and set the date."

"Forgive me, sir," the servant said. "I do not know why." He bowed and left. Then the king sent his spies to find out more. They soon reported the news of the princess who wouldn't marry a turtle.

"What a foolish idea," said the king. "How can she judge you by a name? We will have to change her mind." So Kachba and his father made some plans.

Weeks later, the princess was standing on her balcony when suddenly she the sounds of a wedding march. Great drums beat and fine horns played as hundreds of happy men danced slowly down the road. After them came a magnificent looking groom riding proudly on a white horse well covered with gold.

"Ah, the man shines as much as his horse," sighed the princess. "Look at his kind face. He seems like a god or a king. Who is he?"

"Why that's Kachba, of course," replied her maid. "But I wonder who his lucky bride is?"

"No, no, that can't be Kachba," said the princess. "Kachba is ugly and looks like a turtle because that's his name."

"Well, that man is Kachba," said the maid. "And he certainly doesn't seem like a turtle."

"Is that really, really Kachba?" asked the princess. And when the maid nodded yes, the princess knew she'd made a terrible mistake. But she also knew what to do. She turned to her maid, saying, "Go to the prince. Tell him it is usual to stop in front of the palace."

Minutes later, when the horse had stopped, the princess stepped onto the street. She looked up at Kachba and asked, "If you are Kachba, why are you dressed as a bridegroom?"

"To be married, of course," he replied.

"But you are to marry me," said the princess bravely.

"Who are you?" asked Kachba, although he knew full well.

"I am your bride to be, the princess of this land," she replied.

"No, you can't be my bride," he said. "You refused me because kachba means turtle."

Blushing, the princess bent her head and said, "Do forgive my foolishness. Kachba is only a name, isn't it? And such a nice name, really. Now I like it very much."

The prince laughed then, eager to forgive her, and pleased at her clever reply. The fake wedding march soon turned around, and Kachba hurried home to get ready for his real marriage.

Meanwhile, the entire city prepared for the great event. Flowers like a carpet covered the road, strings of pearls hung happily from rich houses. Lovely lamps filled with fine oils lined the streets. Finally, the two were wed in a ceremony that lasted for days.

After that, they lived joyfully together. And later, when they became king and queen of Kachba's lands, they ruled with great wisdom for a long, long time.

Kolams

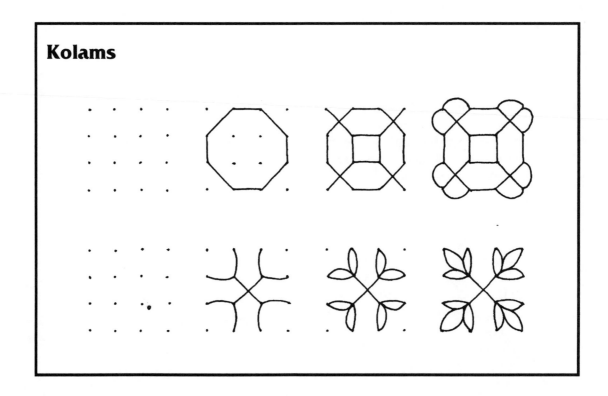

For Further Exploration of India

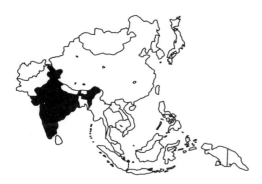

India, officially known as the Republic of India (or Bharat in Hindi); South Asia

Area: 1,222,243 sq. miles

Population: 952,107,694 (1996 est.); 73% rural

Official language: Hindi, with English as an associate language

Largest city: Mumbai (formerly Bombay)

Activity: Kolams

For weddings such as this one, and for festive occasions across India, intricate drawings are made, called by various names, including *kolams*.

Many women daily draw kolams in front of their homes using chalk powder or powdered quartz. On holidays, kolams can creep across streets, often with colors from brick red to modern bright hues. For certain ceremonies and rituals in homes or temples, the kolam is created with rice flour on the floor.

Indian girls often make their own kolam books, carefully noting down favorite designs, from geometric patterns to images and symbols of gods as well as pictures of animals, objects, and flowers.

To make your own

You can use markers or crayons to make kolams either on small papers on tables, or covering large pieces of roll paper spread over the floor. If weather permits, they also look lovely drawn with colored chalk on pavement. Children can try the patterns below and on p. 21 and make their own designs, too, either in a freehand fashion or on grids of dots.

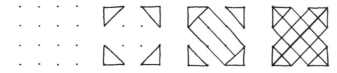

Library/Information Skills Activity

India has an unusual symbol in its national flag, and this can be an excellent opportunity to introduce children to a special reference book found in many school library media centers and public libraries, the *World of Flags* (Chicago: Rand McNally, 1994). If your library doesn't have this or a similar reference book on national flags, you can use a multimedia encyclopedia, such as the Microsoft Encarta Encyclopedia. Show the children how to use the table of contents and the index to locate India's flag, and ask them to find out the name of the symbol. (*Answer:* It is the Buddhist dharma chakra, or wheel of life, used in India for thousands of years.)

Books to Share

India's many different languages, customs, and religions are confusing for children to grasp. The following picture books provide a nice range of images.

Axworthy, Anni. *Anni's India Diary.* New York: Whispering Coyote Press, 1992. A voyage through India in pictures and text.

Hermes, Jules. *The Children of India.* Minneapolis: Carolrhoda Books, 1993.

Haskins, James. *Count Your Way Through India.* Minneapolis: Carolrhoda Books, 1990. An introduction to the land and people of India, accompanied by instruction on how to read and pronounce number one through ten in Hindi.

Jaffrey, Madhur. *Seasons of Splendour.* New York: Atheneum, 1985. A nicely illustrated selection of Indian tales.

Wolf, Gita. *The Very Hungry Lion.* San Diego: Annick Press, 1996. A trickster tale from western India illustrated in the traditional style of Warli folk art.

Chapter 6

Laos

When the river is in flood, the fish eat the ants.
When the river goes dry, the ants eat the fish.

Laos is a small landlocked country much affected by the Vietnam War. Rich in ethnic groups and their stories, Laos is primarily a farming land, where Buddhism is still practiced today, even under Communist rule. Buddhist teachings encourage compassion, charity, and the calm acceptance taught by this tale.

A Dog's Wish

Once in Laos there lived an old dog, who loved to laze in the sun all day. But one morning, he looked up at that bright light and thought, "How nice it would feel to **be** the sun, not just to sit under it."

Indra, the God of Heaven, heard him and decided to grant his wish. Suddenly the dog felt on fire. He seemed to grow bigger and bigger. Then he looked down at the earth below and was most pleased. He was the **sun.** He sent sunbeams down and felt so strong and powerful. Until a cloud came by and covered him all up.

"That huge cloud can hide me completely. I think I'd rather be a cloud," he decided. So Indra granted that wish. The dog was now a cloud. He felt lovely and soft, floating grandly in the sky, riding with the wind. But then the wind grew wild and whipped him roughly around.

"It's better to be the wind," he thought. All at once, he seemed light yet full of speed. Now, as the wind, he blew here and there and loved his new job. Until he hit a tall anthill.

"What a nuisance," he whined. "I am the wind, but I can't move this thing. I'd rather be an anthill standing so proudly."

Indra heard and changed the dog to an anthill. The anthill felt very happy now. He stood firmly and enjoyed all the tiny feet tickling him. But all of a sudden, he felt a great shock. Something huge bumped into him, almost knocking him down. He looked up to see a big water buffalo.

"Ahh, it would be wise to be such a strong animal," he decided and suddenly he was. As a water buffalo, he walked slowly in the sun. He enjoyed cooling baths in the mud. Until a man came one day.

"Time to work," said the man, tying a rope around the animal. Then he pulled the buffalo back and forth across the field.

"I don't like this at all," thought the water buffalo. "It's best to be a man in charge of everything."

Indra, although a little tired, helped once again. The dog now stood on two legs and looked just like a man.

"Hurry home!" cried a woman's voice. The man returned to his house where his wife shared her cares—about the crop, their children, his parents.

"My head aches from thinking and worrying," thought the man to himself. Just then he saw a lazy dog sitting outside.

"How silly I was," he said. "It's no fun to be a man either. I'm best off as a nice, old dog."

At once he could feel his tail wag. He snuggled down, he enjoyed his warm fur. And then he barked loudly with great joy, delighted to be the best thing he could be … himself.

For Further Exploration of Laos

Laos, officially known as the Lao People's Democratic Republic; Southeast Asia
Area: 91,429 sq. miles
Population: 4,975,772 (1996 est.); 80% rural
Official language: Lao
Largest city: Vientiane

Activity: Elephant Mural

Some Lao temple walls have finely painted murals, often depicting scenes from the Buddha's lifetimes, including several as an elephant. Elephants have long been found in Laos, in both forests and royal courtyards. Thus a mural of elephants is a wonderful way to continue your exploration of Laos.

First, help your listeners to imagine the lives and work of Laotian elephants past and present. Mention elephants of old decorated with golden ornaments to hold a king, and elephants hauling logs in the forest, bathing in a river, walking in procession, helping in a temple, or just playing and spraying.

Then enlarge copies of the elephant below and on p. 49 for children to decorate, or have them draw and decorate their own elephants.

Cut out all the elephants and paste on one large piece of roll paper. Then children can color in background details right on the paper. Older children can make setting images on separate pieces of colored paper, then cut and paste them onto the mural. Words can also be added to describe the elephants or to tell a tale of many elephants.

Library/Information Skills Activity

Elephants are fascinating animals to children of any age because of their sheer size and strength. Challenge your children to locate facts about elephants using the nonfiction section of the library. Explain the difference between fiction and nonfiction books, and show them how the nonfiction books are shelved by their Dewey decimal number. Then have them use the library's card or computer catalog to locate books on elephants, and use the Dewey number to locate the books on the shelf.

Books to Share

Unfortunately there are very few picture books about Laos, although there are several on the Hmong people of Laos (see suggestions under chapter 13).

Spagnoli, Cathy. *Thao Kham, the Pebble Shooter.* Bothell, WA: The Wright Group, 1995. A very tellable Lao tale about a disabled boy who becomes a hero.

Chapter 7

Philippines

Behind the mountain of sacrifices,
Lies the valley of success.

In the Philippines are thousands of islands and countless coconuts—it is the world's largest coconut exporter. The Philippines are also home to many Christians, over ninety percent of the population follows that faith. The tales told in the Philippines are of the land and its legends, as well as of heroes, saints, fools, and tricksters. Juan Posong, known under several names, is a favorite trickster. Below two tricks are combined which are often told together. Separate them into two shorter tales, if you wish, for very young listeners.

Juan & His Tricks

Juan Posong lived in the Philippines and played many a trick. He was smart and brave enough to fool even the king. One day, Juan mixed and fixed a cake. Then he walked to the palace and presented the cake to the king. After the king ate the whole cake, he sent for Juan.

"Your cake was extremely delicious. What was its secret ingredient?" he asked. Juan scratched his head, but did not answer.

"I order you to speak up," said the king.

"Your highness," replied Juan. "It is a most unusual ingredient. You may not like it at all."

"Tell me at once!" roared the king.

"Dog's hair," said Juan. "You must add the hair of my dog."

The king frowned. Indeed, that was a strange thing to put in a cake. But the cake was delicious. So the king said, "Bring your dog here tomorrow and you will be rewarded."

Early the next day, Juan returned with his dog and received much gold. The dog was then carefully fed, bathed, and exercised. She lived royally in the palace. After several days, the king felt hungry for a treat and called the palace cook.

"Cut the hairs of that dog and serve them to me," he ordered. "Since they make a cake taste so nice, they must be sweet even when raw."

Eagerly, the cook caught the dog. He brushed her hair and then carefully cut some of it. He washed the hair, dried it in the sun, then served the dog's hair—spread out and glistening on a golden plate. With a greedy grin, the king took a big handful. He put them into his mouth and closed his eyes.

"Uuuucccchhhh," he cried as he as he tried to spit them out. They tasted terrible. They scratched his tongue, tickled his teeth, and stuck like glue to the inside of his mouth.

"I've been tricked," he shouted. "Find that rascal and punish him."

Now Juan had left the city days ago, for he knew that the king's men would soon chase him. When he left, he took pots of food and fled to a far-off beach. There he ate and enjoyed himself. Then one day, he saw a ship coming in, and he thought of another tricky idea.

He dug some deep holes, then buried leftover food in each one. Next he found a frog, a nice big frog. He tied a string to its neck and sat watching it hop and .... hop .... and .... hop.

While the frog was moving about, the ship landed. Soon, the ship's captain came up to Juan. He saw a high jumping frog, and a man whose head went up and down, up and down along with the frog.

"What are you doing?" asked the captain finally.

"Ah, watching my most clever frog. He's a food-finding frog. Right now he's telling me where to dig for dinner," replied Juan. The captain shook his head, asking with a frown, "How could that be?"

Juan replied, "If you don't believe me, why not dig here where the frog suggests? See for yourself."

Strong sailors soon were shoveling sand and, all of a sudden, one cried, "I've hit something!" His friends rushed to help and they pulled out a pot full of fine smells.

"Amazing," gasped the captain as he tasted the food. "How useful this would be for us as we travel. We could simply land anywhere and the frog would find us our lunch or dinner. We wouldn't need to carry much food on our ship anymore. Will you sell him?"

Juan shook his head and said, "I like him too much. And he is very valuable to me."

"Yes, I know," agreed the captain. "I will pay well." And he signaled to his men who brought five bars of gold. Then he asked, "Is this enough?"

"You will never again need to pay for food," Juan reminded him. "Add a little more."

So the captain called for two more bars. Juan agreed and sold the frog. With a smile, he walked away quickly, while the captain followed the frog over the sands. Each time the frog stopped, the captain's men dug and dug and dug.

Yet you and I know that they found nothing at all. Hours later, the captain finally realized that he'd been tricked. He and his men searched everywhere for Juan. But of course, Juan could not be found. He had already reached another town, far away. There he hid his gold, wore a disguise, and happily planned his next trick.

For Further Exploration of the Philippines

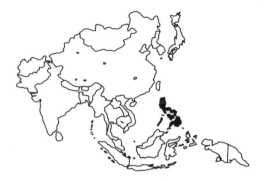

Activity: Riddles

Juan used his wits to trick others. Have listeners use their wits to answer some fun Filipino riddles which describe objects in clever ways. Most answers will be familiar, although the broom is not the tall type used here but the shorter kind used in much of Asia. It is made of broom "straws" tied together and used as the sweeper bends or squats to sweep.

And the coconut is described as it comes from the tree, not as it is sold in American supermarkets—without its outer covering.

Two boats with only one pilot. *(shoes)*

Little brothers and sisters who have only one belt. *(broom)*

Planted in the early afternoon, harvested at dawn. *(stars)*

It is a dangerous telegram for death often is the result. *(gun)*

She wears a crown and has eyes all over. *(pineapple)*

It stands on one leg and has a head but no face. *(mushroom)*

It comes and goes, it blows and blows. *(wind)*

The skin is near the husk, the husk is near the shell, The shell is near the pearl, the pearl is near the water. *(coconut)*

Library/Information Skills Activity

The Philippines have an average temperature of 80 degrees with an average annual rainfall of 80 inches. This might be a good occasion to introduce your children to several sources of current information on weather. Ask them to pick a U.S. city or a major international city, and compare temperature and rainfall there with the Philippines. Any general almanac, such as the *World Almanac*, can be used.

For a real treat, if your school or library has access to the World Wide Web, have them use the URL <http://www.city.net/countries/philippines/> for a current weather forecast. This site can also give you access to a regional view by using </regions/Asia> in place of countries. There are many additional links to information about the region and specific countries that you will see as you scroll down the page.

Books to Share

Aruego, Jose. *Rockabye Crocodile: A Folktale from the Philippines.* New York: Mulberry Books, 1993. A traditional tale of kindness rewarded.

Lucas, Alice, ed. *Mga Kuwentong Bayan. Folk Stories from the Philippines.* San Francisco Study Center, 1995. Bilingual tales.

San Souci, Robert. *Pedro and the Monkey.* New York: Morrow Junior Books, 1996. This is a Filipino version of the classic Puss-in-Boots, but the cat becomes a monkey.

Thailand

Ride an elephant to catch grasshoppers.

The proud country of Thailand stayed almost completely free from colonial rule in recent times, when much of Asia did not. It remains a friendly, peaceful land rich in various art forms. The Buddhist religion is followed by most Thai people, and the temple is a center of activity. Although industry is rapidly developing in Thailand, many farms and villages sit peacefully still near countryside temples. In such surroundings, this story might be told.

Watching the Garden

Once in Thailand, a little boy was sent to watch the garden. But after a while he grew bored and went off to play. As soon as he left, a crow swooped down and stole some beans. Just then, the boy's grandfather came and was most annoyed. After some time, the boy returned with a smile, which quickly turned to a frown when he saw his grandfather's face.

"Look what happened when you left," the old man said to the boy. "We need those beans. You should have watched. It was your work." The boy felt very sad and wanted to help. He decided to get the beans back from the crow. So he ran to a hunter and said, "Please, sir. Shoot an arrow at that crow so he will drop the beans he stole."

"Why should I bother the crow?" asked the hunter. "You made the mistake." The boy walked on until he found a mouse.

"Please, little mouse," he said. "Chew the hunter's bowstrings so he'll shoot an arrow for me."

"I'm not mad at the hunter," said the mouse. "It's your problem."

So the boy walked on. Soon he saw a cat and said, "Please, friend cat, nip that mouse so it will help me." But the cat, too, refused, so the boy found a dog.

"Dear dog," he said. "Chase that cat so it will nip the mouse and help me."

"Chase him yourself," replied the dog. "I'm busy." Then the boy found a hammer and begged him to beat the dog.

"I'm too tired," sighed the hammer. So the boy ran to a fire.

"Fire, strong fire," he said. "Burn that stubborn hammer so it will agree."

"Too much work," sizzled the fire. Next the boy pleaded with some water, "Pour yourself on the fire, dear water, to help me."

"But I like that fire," replied the water. So the boy asked the earth to cover the water, but the earth refused too. Then the boy found an elephant and begged, "Could you please pound the earth so it will cover the water."

The elephant shook his trunk so the boy sat down and cried. When he did, a little gnat flew around him. Suddenly he caught it.

"Now, little gnat," he said. "Fly into the elephant's ear and annoy him, or I'll squeeze you to death."

The gnat was scared. He flew into the elephant's ear.

The elephant pounded the earth.

The earth covered the water.

The water fell on the fire.

The fire burned the hammer.

The hammer threatened the dog.

The dog chased the cat.

The cat nipped the mouse.

The mouse bit the bowstring.

The hunter shot an arrow.

The arrow scared the crow.

The crow dropped the beans.

And they fell right into the garden again.

The grandfather was delighted and forgave the boy at once. Then they enjoyed a meal of the best noodles and the freshest vegetables. But after that, the boy always watched the garden very, very carefully. And he waited until he was all finished before he went to play.

For Further Exploration of Thailand

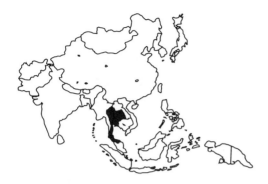

Thailand, formerly Siam, officially the Kingdom of
  Thailand; Southeast Asia
Area: 198,115 sq. miles
Population: 58,851,357 (1996 est.); 75% rural
Official language: Thai, with English used for com-
  merce and government
Largest city: Bangkok

Activity: Making a Basket (to hold garden vegetables!)

The Thai are famous for their basketry, so from the Thai exhibit at the wonderful Seattle Children's Museum comes a simple way for young children to make a basket.

Materials: five 1" x 12" tagboard strips, yarn, vines, cloth scraps, stapler, scissors, tape or glue.

1. Take four of the strips and arrange them so that they cross evenly. Staple through the center.

2. Take the remaining strip and staple into a ring, overlapping ends about ½".

3. Push the four crossed strips through the ring, forming basket shape. Glue or tape strips to the ring.

4. Fold over the tops of the strips and secure.

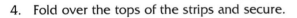

5. Weave yarn, twine, cloth in and out around sides. Then go shopping!

Library/Information Skills Activity

Thailand is a constitutional monarchy. This might be a good occasion to introduce your children to some of the general reference books in the library, such as the Universal Almanac or the World Almanac, that list the heads of state. Show the children where to find the almanacs, and how to use the tables of contents and indexes to locate information. Then ask them to locate the name of the current King of Thailand. (Answer: King Bhumibol Adulyadej)

Books to Share

Hamada, Cheryl. *Kao and the Golden Fish: A Folktale from Thailand.* Danbury, CT: Children's Press, 1994.

Ho, Minfong. *Hush! A Thai Lullaby.* New York: Orchard Books, 1996. A lovely picture book with Thai sounds and images that was selected as a Caldecott Medal Honor book in 1997.

Meeker, Clare. *A Tale of Two Rice Birds.* Seattle: Sasquatch Books, 1994. A nicely illustrated Thai folktale.

Oliviera, James. *Som See and the Magic Elephant.* New York: Hyperion, 1995. Som See discovers a magic elephant to help her great-aunt's journey.

Chapter 9

Nepal

Garland of gold to the listener, garland of flowers to the teller.
May this tale go to heaven and come down to be told again.
Traditional ending

Nepal is a beautiful land with both the awesome Himalayas and ancient valleys. Hindu and Buddhist religions coexist very peacefully, and festivals are many in this land of hardworking, simple living people. With so many deities to worship, also come many demons and monsters to fear, a fact which some clever women used well in this tale.

We Want Rice

Once in Nepal, a mother, father, five sons, and their five wives all lived in a big farmhouse. And each one worked very hard every day. But the mother was a stingy type. Although they had several barns full of good rice, she never let anyone eat it.

She only cooked the cheapest food, a paste boiled from corn flour, for every meal. Day after day, the sons and their wives went out to the fields and worked long hours. Yet every night when they returned so hungry, they were given just this rough food. At last, the five wives grew very angry.

"She has so much rice, but we never taste any," the eldest complained.

"If she won't share," said the youngest and most clever, "then we must take the food ourselves."

"But she will find out and punish us," warned another wife.

"Don't worry, I have a plan," replied the youngest.

So the next day while the mother napped, the wives crawled under the biggest barn. Gently they pushed up a floorboard, crept into the barn, and took some rice. They carried it out to the fields where they husked it, boiled it, and enjoyed each warm, delicious grain. Then, very quietly, they put back the empty rice husks.

The following day, they took some rice to the market, sold it, and bought nice vegetables and *dal* (lentils) to cook with it.

Week after week, month after month passed with such secret feasting. But at last, all of the rice in the biggest barn had been eaten.

"We must do something soon or we will be discovered," the wives whispered to each other, suddenly afraid.

"This is what we can do," said the youngest. She told them her plan and everyone agreed. Late that night, they crawled out of bed, then put on strange looking make-up and old clothes. They now appeared very different and rather frightening. Next each one picked up a pan or a drum. And suddenly a great noise sounded in the house.

"Feed us! Feed us! We want rice!" screamed scary voices as drums and banging sounds were heard.

"Husband, wake up," said the mother. "Who is making such an awful noise?" They shivered under the blankets as they heard bodies moving through the house. They peeked out to see fierce monsters dancing wildly. Then, again, they heard loud and terrible voices crying, ***"Feed us now!"***

The two felt too scared to move. They called out, "Take rice, take rice. As much as you like, from the big barn."

More beats and shrieks were heard, then the sounds of loud footsteps going to the barn. At last it was silent. The parents still couldn't sleep. They hid in their bed until birds welcomed dawn.

When everyone was up, the mother asked the daughters-in-law, "Did you hear monsters last night?" The wives tried not to laugh as they answered. A few said they heard something but were too scared to check. Others said that they slept without hearing a sound.

The old couple then went to the biggest barn. They found only empty husks, all the rice was gone.

"See, you silly woman," said her husband. "For many years you were too stingy and never gave anyone a good meal. Now all of this rice is gone. We never enjoyed it. Those monsters ate every grain up."

The old woman felt very sorry and sad. "I was wrong," she admitted. "From now on, we'll all enjoy good food, and leave nothing for greedy monsters."

So from that day on, the old mother was very generous. She cooked rice, dal, and fine vegetables. The good food gave everybody strength to work harder and harder. So the family became quite wealthy. Everyone lived together in peace, and the wives never, ever had to sneak food again.

For Further Exploration of Nepal

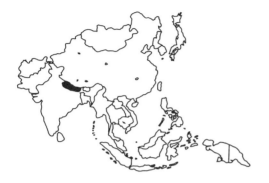

Nepal, officially known as the Kingdom of Nepal; South Asia

Area: 56,136 sq. miles

Population: 21,560,869 (1995 est.); 90% rural

Official language: Nepali

Largest city: Kathmandu

Activity: Lotus Cards

The lotus is an important symbol in both Hinduism and Buddhism, Nepal's two major religions. It is a flower beloved for its purity, along with its beauty, since it emerges from murky waters to bloom so brilliantly. In both religions, it is associated with various deities as well, while it is also found in legends, and given as an offering.

The lovely design of the lotus is often carved or painted in Nepal. It can be made here into a card for children to share with their family, or to send a far away friend.

Copy and enlarge the lotus flower design below to fit across the bottom half of a plain or lightly colored 8 ½" X 11" sheet of paper, one per child.

Have each child fold back the top part of her card, so that the lotus is on the front cover. The lotus can then be painted, colored with crayons, covered with pasted shiny paper bits, or even sprinkled with glitter.

Library/Information Skills Activity

Eight of the ten highest mountains in the world are located in Nepal, including Mt. Everest. Introduce younger children to the atlases and the globe in the school or public library, and show them how major physical features like mountains are identified. For older children, ask them to find Nepal in the atlas, and see if they can identify the tallest mountains on the map.

Books to Share

Since there are so few picture books on Nepal, try this lovely collection, with color photos, cultural background, and fifteen tales:

Shrestha, Kavita Ram and Sarah Lamstein. *From the Mango Tree and Other Folktales from Nepal.* Englewood, CO: Libraries Unlimited, Inc., 1997.

Another useful book:

Pitkanen, Matti A. *The Children of Nepal.* Minneapolis: Carolrhoda Books, 1990.

Chapter 10

Korea

Even a sheet of paper weighs less if four hands lift.

Korea is a country which has lived through tremendous change of late. After Korea's too many invasions and occupations over the years, the Korean War in the early 1950s brought even more death and tragedy. It also left a country sadly divided, with thousands of families separated. Today, although North Korea is weak economically, South Korea has moved forward to become a leader in Asia. Yet even as Korea changes, certain traditional values are still passed on. One such value is that of filial piety, nurtured through tales like this.

The Green Frog

Once there lived a young green frog who was a very naughty little frog. He never, ever did what his mother said. He always did exactly the opposite.

If his mother said, "Sit down now,"
he would jump as high as he could.

If his mother said, "Try catching some flies,"
his mouth snapped shut.

If she said, "Hop over here,"
he would hop over there.

One day, she tried to teach him how to croak.
"Now say *kaegul, kaegul*," she said. But of course he did the opposite and happily croaked, "*kulgae, kulgae.*"

This poor froggy mother, even though she loved her little son, never had an easy moment. She worked very hard until at last her son was all grown up and catching his own flies.

Happily, the mother frog relaxed a little and just sat in the sun. But one day, she grew very ill and knew that she would soon change worlds. Now the frog did not mind dying, since she had lived a long life for a frog. But she did want to be buried in the right place. For to be buried well, in a place of good fortune, is important indeed in Korea. So she looked and looked all around and finally found a perfect spot, on top of a lovely hill.

"But," she thought to herself. "If I tell my son to bury me on top of the hill, he will surely bury me at the bottom, near the river. And my body might slip into the water when it rains and be lost forever. So … I shall tell him to bury me at the bottom of the hill, and he'll bury me at the top. *Good! Good!*"

Well pleased with herself, she called for her son. "My dear, you've been a good little froggy … most of the time," she said. "I love you and I know you will do what I ask. After I die, please, please bury me at the bottom of the hill. At the bottom of the hill," she repeated.

"Yes, mother. Yes, I promise. At the bottom, at the bottom," croaked her son. And soon after that, the mother frog died, well satisfied. But her son was suddenly very sad. He regretted all the trouble he had caused her.

"I wasn't always the best son," he sighed. "I made her work too hard. But I know what I can do to make up for it. This time, I'll do exactly what she asked me to do, and not the opposite. *Yes,* yes, I will." And soon after, he gave his mother a fine funeral and carefully buried her at the *bottom* of the hill, right near the river—just as she told him to do.

But when the rains began to fall, he grew worried. "My mother's body may slide down the bank, fall into the river, get lost, or float to the sea," he thought. "How terrible." With a great unhappy heart, he started to croak just the way his mother used to croak, *"Kaegul, kaegul, kaegul, kaegul."* Soon his relatives heard his sorrowful cries and asked, "Why are you so sad?"

"I was good too late," he cried. "I finally did just what my mother said to do, but it was wrong. Now her body may slide into the river and be lost in the sea. Poor mommy." And those frogs felt sad to think of her poor dead body bouncing around in the waves. So they cried, too, *"Kaegul, kaegul."*

The next time it rained, the frog and all his relatives croaked sadly again, *"Kaegul, kaegul."* So the frogs down the river hopped over to ask why. When they heard the sorry tale, they began to croak as well, *"Kaegul, kaegul."* And the next time it rained, even more frogs heard the story and sang sadly too.

Even today, all those frogs still croak their mournful cries whenever it rains. So if sometime you go to that hill by the river, and hear their sad cries, you will now know why.

rabbit

elephant

For Further Exploration of Korea

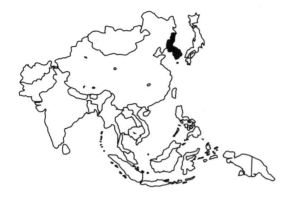

Korea, since 1948, divided into two parts: North Korea, known as the Democratic People's Republic of Korea; and South Korea, known as the Republic of Korea; Northeast Asia

Area: North Korea: 46,549 sq. miles; South Korea: 38,328 sq. miles

Population: North Korea: 23,904,124 (1996 est.) 64% urban; South Korea: 44,606,1995 (1995 est.) 84% urban.

Official language: Korean

Largest cities: P'yongyang (North Korea)
Seoul (South Korea)

Activity: Sound words & language

The frog's cries in the story can be used to introduce a few other Korean sounds. Students learning to read English, with its phonetic challenges, may be surprised to hear how easy it is to learn the very practical Korean alphabet, Han-gul.

It was created in the fifteenth century by a group of scholars under the leadership of the great King Sejong. This simple system was designed as an alternative to the thousands of Chinese characters used by Korean scholars, thus offering literacy for the first time to most of the population.

Try saying a few Korean words and, if possible, have the children try to write a few, too!

Animal name	Animal sounds	Han-gul
dog: *gae*	*mong mong*	개
cat: *goh yahng ee*	*yaong, yaong*	고양이
frog: *kaeguri*	*kaegul, kaegul*	개구리

Greetings

hello: *yoboseyo*

thank you: *kamsa hamnida*

cry of pain: *aigo*

counting 1–5: h*anna, dool, set, net, tasok*

Pronunciation hints: "a" as ah, "e" as in bet, "o" as oh, "u" as oo, "ai" as I, "ao" as ow, "ae" as in day, "i" as ee.

Library/Information Skills Activity

The Internet contains all sorts of useful information, even for primary age children. If your school or library has access to the Internet and the World Wide Web, illustrate what it has to offer by trying these two websites on frogs:

The Froggy Page URL:
<http://frog.simplenet.com/froggy/> activities and information on frogs, from the silly to the scientific.

Frogland URL:
<**http://www.teleport.com/~dstroy/frogland.html**> Facts and fun all focused on frogs.

Books to Share

Choi, Sook Nyul. *The Year of the Impossible Goodbyes.* New York: Houghton Mifflin, 1991. A tale of a 10-year-old's journey from North Korea to South Korea during the Second World War.

De Zutter, Hank. *Who Says a Dog Goes Bow-wow?* New York: Doubleday, 1993. A fine multicultural picture book of animal sounds.

Schecter, Ellen. *Sim Chung and the River Dragon.* New York: Bank Street, 1993. A simple version of Korea's best known tale of filial piety.

Chapter 11

Indonesia

There is no ivory that is not cracked.

Indonesia, with over 13,000 islands, is also home to a very large Muslim population. Each part of Indonesia has its own favorite legends and tales, although some characters, like the trickster mousedeer Kanchil, may be found more widely. Si Kabayan is a human trickster well loved in West Java. Like many tricksters, he is sometimes shown as a fool, and has brains enough to know when to retreat.

A Stranger

Si Kabayan was a farmer who lived on his wits in long ago Java.
Ever ready with a clever answer,
he talked and tricked his way through life.

Now Si Kabayan had a fine water buffalo.
He was so proud of that animal.
Every day in the morning, he walked the buffalo out to his field.
Every night, he brought the buffalo home,
brushed him carefully, even sang him a song.

One afternoon as usual, Si Kabayan returned after lunch to his field.
But his water buffalo was gone.

"Who stole my buffalo?" he bellowed.
Searching round, he found some footprints.
Next to the footprints, he found a handkerchief.

"The thief dropped his handkerchief," shouted Si Kabayan.
"I'll find out whose this is and tear him apart!"
His neighbors soon heard of the theft, and gathered round to help.

"I know that handkerchief," said one man.
"It belongs to the stranger who just moved here."

"And where does this buffalo robber live?" asked Si Kabayan.

"He stays in a house near the river," the man replied.

"I'll teach him a lesson, I will," raged Si Kabayan.
"I'll twist his thieving arm. I'll shake his sneaky shoulders.
I'll pick him up and throw him down, the rat!"

In this furious mood he stomped to the stranger's house.
There in the yard, he saw his buffalo tied up.

"Come out! Come out at once!" he yelled fiercely. He waved the handkerchief to show he knew who stole his buffalo.

At first there was no answer. The house looked very quiet.
Si Kabayan called again in anger, ***"Hurry up! Are you scared?"***

Only the birds sounded in reply.
Si Kabayan shouted once more, ***"I'm waiting and I'm mad!"***
Finally, the stranger stepped out. Si Kabayan was very, very quiet.

For the stranger was ***H-u-g-e!***
His head was as big as a melon.
His muscles were large and hard like coconuts.
His legs were as thick as big banana plants.
"Why are you mad, little man?" he roared, louder than ten elephants.

"Oh, I'm … I'm mad at myself for bothering you,"
whispered Si Kabayan, who was quite small and not too strong.

"That's my handkerchief," shouted the giant. ***"Why do you have it?"***

"I … I … I found it," said Si Kabayan.
"You dropped it in my field, right where my nice buffalo, that was stolen, used to stand. So I … I … I wanted to return it to you."

"Thank you," growled the stranger and snatched it away.

"You are most welcome. Anytime," said Si Kabayan bowing again and again as the giant man walked back in his house.
Then Si Kabayan ran away as fast as his short legs would let him.

Later, his friends came to visit and asked,
"Did you beat up that thief?"

Si Kabayan just grinned and said, "Not exactly. But I told him I was mad. And when I get a little stronger, he'll be ***very, very*** sorry he stole my buffalo!"

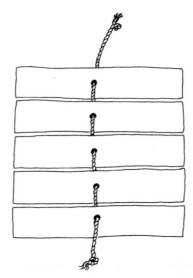

For Further Exploration of Indonesia

Indonesia, officially known as the Republic of Indonesia; Southeast Asia
Area: 13,700 islands comprising 705,192 sq. miles
Population: 194,754,800 (1995 est.); 70% rural
Official language: Bahasa Indonesia
Largest city: Jakarta

Activity: Bookmaking

Indonesia has many wonderful arts and crafts. One interesting art is the making of the traditional books, which unfold and fold like Venetian blinds. They usually have bamboo covers and palm leaf pages inscribed with the tip of a kris, a knifelike weapon cherished in parts of Southeast Asia.

You can adapt the idea by using stiff pieces of paper or cardboard, crayons or markers, a hole punch, and yarn:

1. Give each child five strips of tagboard, roughly 2" X 9". See sample on p. 39.

2. Punch, or have children punch, one hole in the center of each.

3. Have children spread out strips, long sides touching, so that all can be seen. Now children can decorate the strips. Since they are narrow strips, younger children can just color them as they wish. Older children might try drawing objects from a story or writing a few simple words to make a folding story book.

4. Keeping the pictures in order, thread a piece of yarn through the strips as shown on p. 39. Make sure that both ends are knotted or have something attached so that they won't simply pull through the last hole on either end.

5. The book can then be folded together and the yarn looped around to keep the book nicely closed until someone wants to open it up, spread it out, and read it!

Library/Information Skills Activity

Indonesia is a very tropical nation which is home to over 40,000 varieties of flowering plants, including 5,000 different kinds of orchids. For younger children, introduce them to some of the books in the library that contain photographs of flowers, and show them what an orchid looks like. For older children, ask them to use the library card or computer catalog to determine whether the library has any books on orchids. If it does, have them locate some photographs or drawings of orchids. If not, have them look under the broader subject heading "flowers."

Books to Share

Boegehold, Betty. *Small Deer's Magic Tricks.* New York: Coward, McCann & Geoghegan, 1977. A book about the famous Indonesian trickster, Kanchil, the mousedeer.

Morton, James. *Komodo Dragons: Giant Lizards of Indonesia.* New York: Capstone, 1995.

Spagnoli, Cathy. *Kantjil and Tiger.* Bothell, WA: The Wright Group, 1995. Another story about this popular Indonesian trickster.

Chapter 12

Vietnam

One little worm can spoil a pot of soup.

Vietnam is a land with a difficult past. It has suffered many wars over the years and been at times under the rule of the Chinese as well as the French. But there have also been periods of proud independence. From both years of struggle and pride come great and revered heroes. Here is a boyhood legend of one such leader.

Dinh Tien Hoang

Long, long ago in the beautiful country of Vietnam there lived a little boy named Dinh Tien Hoang. He was a very clever boy who stayed with his uncle since his parents had died. His job was to watch the water buffaloes.

Every day he took them to the field and met his friends there, who also watched their family buffaloes. The animals would find some cool mud and sit peacefully while the boys played with stones and bamboo. They ate their tasty sticky rice, then told stories as they rested. It was a good life.

One day, Dinh said, "Why don't we play king? Let's choose a king and soldiers." This was an exciting new game and the boys happily agreed. Since Dinh was the smartest and the bravest, they all thought that he should be king. He was well pleased and decided to celebrate.

"We will have a feast," he declared, "and enjoy some roasted meat." So very carefully the boys lit a fire, then killed and cooked one of Dinh's buffaloes. It made a grand feast. They ate and ate and ate. But then, too soon, the sun slipped down. It was time to go home. All the boys ran off, their stomachs full. But Dinh looked at the buffaloes and grew worried.

"My uncle will be so mad," he thought. "What can I do?" He stared again at the animals and all of a sudden, he had a plan. He cut off the tail left from the buffalo they had eaten and buried most of it in the ground. A little bit of tail stuck up into the air. With a smile, he returned home, herding the other buffaloes back. At the gate, his uncle counted the animals.

"One is missing. Where is he?" asked the uncle.

"Dear uncle," replied Dinh. "He decided to go exploring underground."

"What nonsense is that?" the uncle demanded.

"Come, I will show you," said the boy, and he led his uncle to the field. There, in the moonlight, he showed him the tail peeking out of the earth.

"Look, uncle, he entered the ground right there. You can see only his tail now, he's almost gone." The uncle marched over and pulled the tail. He fell back hard on the ground, holding the little piece in his hand.

"You bad child," he cried as Dinh began to run away. "Wait until I catch you."

Dinh ran quickly to the river, where his friend Dragon the ferryman lived. He called his name as he ran, *"Help Dragon, help."*

But the ferryman didn't answer, he was in a deep sleep. Instead, a fierce and mighty dragon soared out from his home at the river bottom. Looking most splendid, he arched his back, stretched his wings and flew right to Dinh, bowing before him.

Dinh, although surprised, didn't wait to ask questions. He jumped on the dragon's back and they crossed the river. His uncle stopped when he saw the dragon. He watched in amazement as the dragon bowed to the boy, then carried him proudly. Suddenly he knew that this boy was indeed someone most special.

The uncle walked slowly home, thinking about what he had seen. Much later, Dinh returned but he was not punished. He lived quietly after that, working and studying every day, and helping his uncle as well. Thus he grew into a very brave and famous leader of the Vietnamese people, King Dinh Tien Hoang.

For Further Exploration of Vietnam

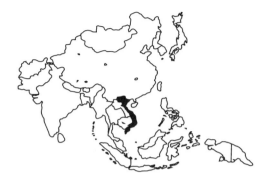

Vietnam, officially known as the Socialist Republic
of Vietnam; Southeast Asia
Area: 127,301 sq. miles
Population: 73,976,973 (1996 est.)
Language: Vietnamese
Largest city: Ho Chi Minh City (formerly Saigon)

Activity: Game

Just as Dinh Tien Hoang enjoyed games with his
friends, your students may like to try this Vietnamese
game collected by Cliff Sloane.

De De Ùm (Ye Ye Um!)

One person, the "Catcher," holds her hand palm up.
The other players gather around, each one points a
forefinger at the Catcher's palm. The Catcher calls out
slowly, *"De De Ùm."* At the sound of the last word, the
Catcher tries to grab a finger of any player. The first
caught is It and has to stand in the center of the room,
in Its territory. That territory is a narrow rectangle going
across room, about one foot by the width of room. The
Catcher stands at one end of room with the others.

Children must then run across room and touch
"base"— an object already decided upon. Next, they
crouch down and cross arms to hold opposite
earlobes. In this position, they have to return across
room to safety.

Of course, It tries to catch children as they cross Its
territory. Older children can try to use strategy to
distract or confuse It. Whoever is caught becomes the
next Catcher and game starts again.

Library/Information Skills Activity

Use the dragon in this story to illustrate the difference
between fiction and nonfiction books. Demonstrate the
difference by contrasting the fictional dragon with
dinosaurs. Compare the real and made up creatures
using books from your collection. Talk to children about
the different locations for each type of material in your
library. Then have children search the library catalog
using key words and locate the materials they have
found.

Books to Share

Breckler, Rosemary. *Sweet Dried Apples: A
Vietnamese Wartime Childhood.* New York:
Houghton Mifflin, 1996. A young Vietnamese girl
narrates a brief bittersweet tale of village childhood during the final stages of the war.

Garland, Sherry. *The Lotus Seed.* New York: Voyager,
1997. The tale of a young girl who took a seed
from the Imperial Garden in Vietnam, and how it
influenced her life.

Lee, Jeanne M. *Toad is the Uncle of Heaven: A
Vietnamese Folk Tale.* New York: Henry Holt,
1989. Toad goes to heaven to end a drought.
Parents' Choice Honor Award.

Palazzo, Janet. *Tam's Slipper: A Story from Vietnam.*
New York: Troll, 1997.

Shalant, Phillis. *Look What We've Brought You From
Vietnam.* New York: Julian Messner, 1988. The
dragon is a popular figure in Vietnamese folklore
and one which children also love. You can find
directions for making dragon puppets (and much
more) from Vietnam in this book.

Chapter 13

Hmong

Able to weave, don't waste thread,
Able to speak, don't waste words.

The Hmong have lived proudly in the mountains of Laos for centuries. But after they helped the American army in Laos, they were forced to flee. Many resourceful Hmong refugees have shared their traditional skills of needlework and farming with new neighbors in the U.S., working very hard. Here is a favorite legend, with a refrain children like to join in on, to help remind listeners that hard work is always best!

The Corn & the Lazy Farmer

Once there was a farmer in Laos who didn't like to work hard. He only liked to sleep and dream. But at last he grew hungry from resting too much, so he decided to plant some corn.

The next day, he walked to the field. He cut down a few small trees.
He smoothed the ground. Then he took some corn seed.
He threw it down to the right, to the left.
But soon the sun was so bright and he was so tired.
He returned home to sleep and later, tiny corn plants burst out of the soil.

Day by day, the sun helped the corn to grow.
Day by day, the rain helped the corn to grow.
Day by day, the corn grew higher and higher.
But the weeds all round also grew higher and higher and higher.

Soon the weeds began to hurt the corn.
The corn called out loudly,
"Mr. Farmer, Mr. Farmer, please come help us.
The weeds are hurting us. They won't let us grow."

The lazy farmer was resting in the sun near his house.
He heard the corn and called back, "All right, all right.
I'll come soon. Tell the weeds to stop!"

The corn waved proudly at the weeds and said,
"Our farmer is coming soon. Stop hurting us or he'll pull you out!"

The weeds were not scared. They felt too strong.
Early the next day, a dog ran to the field.

"Is that your master?" asked the weeds.

"No," said the corn. "Our master has a big hat, a pipe, and a long knife."

So the weeds kept choking the corn.
The next day, a chicken hopped to the field.

"Is that your master?" asked the weeds.

"No," said the corn. "Our master has a big hat, a pipe, and a long knife."

So the weeds kept hurting the corn.
The next day, a tiger growled near the field.

"Is that your master?" asked the weeds.

"No," the corn said. "Our master has a big hat, a pipe, and a long knife."

So the weeds pressed more tightly around the corn.
The next day, a snake slithered across the field.

"Is that your master?" asked the weeds.

"No," said the corn. "Our master has a big hat, a pipe, and a long knife."

So the weeds kept wrapping round the poor corn.
Finally, the farmer came to the field. He wore a big hat.
He had a pipe in his mouth and a long knife in his belt.

"Is that your master?" asked the weeds.

"Yes," cried the corn happily.
And the farmer pulled out all the big weeds.
The corn felt wonderful. Now each plant had room to breathe.
They were all so pleased that they told the farmer, "Go and clean your house. Make a nice place for us and we will come to you. You won't even have to pick us."

But the tired farmer just went home and fell asleep.
A week passed, and still he loafed and lazed.
Finally, the corn was nice and big. All the plants pulled themselves out of the ground and bounced over to the farmer's house.

"Open the door," they called.
But they heard only a loud snore.
They pushed the door open and saw the sleeping farmer.
They saw a messy house with no clean place for them.
The plants were so mad that they turned and bounced back to the field.
They jumped quickly into the ground and decided never to leave again.

So, ever since that day, corn won't come to my house or to your house or to anybody's home.
Someone, somewhere, has to go to a cornfield and pick it.
All because of that lazy, lazy farmer.

For Further Exploration of the Hmong

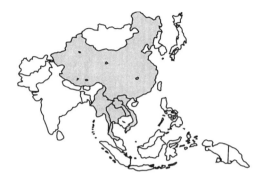

Hmong, a minority group located primarily in China and Southeast Asia

Area: Located in China, Vietnam, Laos, Thailand, and Myanmar (Burma)

Population: An estimated 300,000-600,000 live in the five nations.

Official language: Hmong

Activity: Hmong Story Cloths

The Hmong are known for their beautiful embroidered textiles. Their sewn story cloths are especially interesting because they tell stories of daily life or from folklore. Share the images in the books listed in Books to Share, then make a story cloth with your students.

With young children, you can decide together the characters and setting of the story you wish to use on a story cloth; older children might like to make their own choices. To create a simple story cloth, use large pieces of roll paper (cut in widths of about 2'). Younger children can draw crayon or marker pictures of story scenes and characters directly on light colored paper. Children able to cut enjoy cutting and pasting story images from colored paper onto a piece of dark roll paper.

The Hmong cloths have lovely borders, often of triangles, like mountains, one after another. If children wish, they can work on an outside border as well.

When the story cloth is done, have children take turns telling their stories. It is an excellent way for children to try storytelling in a non-threatening manner. The images are there to help the child remember the story. And if very young tellers begin to ramble or get stuck, a kind teacher can gently bring them back by referring to the cloth's pictures.

This project can also be done well in small groups, or as a whole class project, with each child contributing one image to be pasted on a large story cloth.

Library/Information Skills Activity

Read *Dia's Story Cloth* to children. Then share other stories about how people have used textiles to tell and remember their stories. Possibilities include: *Sweet Clara and the Freedom Quilt* by Deborah Hopkinson (Knopf, 1993), *The Keeping Quilt* by Patricia Polacco (Simon & Schuster, 1988), and *Tar Beach* by Faith Ringgold (Crown, 1991).

To see a lovely collection of Hmong textile designs, go to the Southeast Asian Archive.
<http://www.lib.uci.edu/sea/hmong.html/>

Books to Share

Cha, Dia. *Dia's Story Cloth.* New York: Lee and Low Books, 1996. Based on a traditional Hmong story cloth, it relates the story of the author's family journey from Laos to the United States.

Shea, Pegi Deitz, Anita Riggio, and You Yang. *The Whispering Cloth: A Refugee's Story.* Honesdale, PA: Boyds Mill Press, 1995.

Xiong, Blia and Cathy Spagnoli. *Nine-In-One, Grr! Grr!* San Francisco: Children's Book Press, 1989. This legend tells why not many tigers live on earth today. ALA Notable now also on CD-ROM.

Chapter 14

Sri Lanka

The tortoise cried, "No, No," when sentenced to be thrown in the water.

The beautiful island of Sri Lanka, though still troubled by internal strife, is one rich in the folklore of both the Sinhalese and the Tamil people who live there. The majority of people are Buddhist, and the Buddhist birth stories, the Jataka tales, are widely told. This is a Jataka story which also features a fierce South Asian monster, the *rakshasa*.

The Pond

Long ago, a monkey king lived with his followers in a quiet woods. One day, after they moved to a new part of the forest, he gathered them together.

"My friends," he said. "This is our home and a good one it will be. But you must take care. Some of the berries here are poisonous. Please show me what you pick before you eat it. Then I can teach you which ones are good and which ones to avoid. And when you get thirsty, you must also be careful. There are many lovely lakes and ponds with good clear water. But in a few ponds live some very bad monsters, *rakshasas* (monsters) who would love to eat you up. Always check carefully before you drink from a pond. If you notice anything strange, call me."

All the monkeys nodded monkey heads, scratched monkey fur, then scurried away. Day after happy day, they played in the forest. They ate the good berries, they drank from safe ponds. But one day, a small group played and jumped for hours in the sun. Soon, they grew hot and longed for a drink. They searched and searched for water and at last found a beautiful calm pond.

"Oh, I'm so thirsty, mommy," said one little monkey. "I'm going to dive in and drink and drink." He hopped right toward the water.

"Wait!" cried his mother and with a leap, she caught him, then held him close. "Let us check first."

The other monkeys glanced around. They became a little afraid. Although the pond looked all right, it seemed almost too calm, too quiet. Their monkey hairs started to shiver, they felt as if someone or something was watching them.

"I don't like it here, but my baby is so thirsty," said another mother. "What should we do?"

"Let us ask the king, just to be sure," decided the oldest monkey there. Someone was sent at once to find the king. He came quickly and went to the edge of the pond. There he noticed many, many footsteps. But all of the footsteps pointed just one way—into the pond.

"You were right to call me," he said. "See how many footsteps go into the pond. But not one comes back out. This is the home of a rakshasa." Then the brave king called out, ***"You can't fool us, you mean monster! We won't come into your pond to die!"***

Suddenly a horrid creature rose out of the water. It had several heads, bulging eyes, huge teeth, and large claws.

"You stupid monkey!" shouted the rakshasa. ***"You ruined my supper. I was just about to eat some good monkey meat. Well at least you'll never drink my water! I hope you die of thirst!!"***

But the monkey king was clever. He looked around the pond and saw fine large bamboo growing. So he called to the monkeys, "Pick good long bamboos. Check that they are hollow inside. Then each of you hold one and find a place near the pond." The monkeys happily picked the bamboo, then circled the pond. Each held a bamboo that reached all the way to the water.

"All right, Rakshasa. Now watch us. Just because you are big, doesn't mean you are clever," cried the monkey king. And he told the monkeys to put their bamboo into the pond, then to have a nice delicious drink.

With big grins, the monkeys used their giant straws to have long, long drinks. And the rakshasa could only shout and splash angrily. He couldn't stop them. For one small monkey's wisdom beat a monster's great size and strength.

For Further Exploration of Sri Lanka

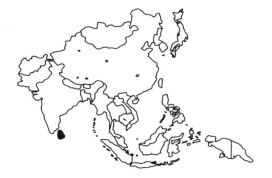

Sri Lanka, formerly Ceylon; South Asia
Area: 25,332 sq. miles
Population: 18,553,074 (1996 est.); 75% rural
Official language: Sinhalese
Largest city: Columbo

Activity: Riddles

In Sri Lanka, stories like this are told for many reasons; one reason is to sharpen wits. Riddles, of course, serve the same purpose. Here are a few from Sri Lanka to try.

The hardest riddle is the last, for it evokes a strong picture of rural Sri Lanka, where the sambur (Indian elk) might graze in the forest and the crocodile, lurking in nearby waters, would be held in both awe and fear, just like a king.

These riddles let children see that some things, like the moon or a candle, are very much the same all over the world. And other things, like the sambur or the crocodile, are not.

Fruit on a tree, tree on a fruit. *(Pineapple)*

The flower that blooms over the mountain head,
The flower that blooms when we are in bed.
(Moon)

The lady who sheds tears all the time.
(Candle)

A mat which stretches and stretches and stretches, but you can't see the end. *(Road)*

An animal with two tails. *(Elephant)*

Who makes the sound, "tan tan?"
Who makes the sound, "tin tin?"
Who throws sand on the road?
Who is king of two villages?

(The sambur makes the sound "tan tan."
The squirrel makes the sound "tin tin."
The cock throws sand on the road.
The crocodile is king of two villages.)

Library/Information Skills Activity

Have the children make a list of monsters, like the rakshasa in this story. Then show them how to use the library card or computer catalog to search by subject for books on these monsters. Challenge them to find as many different books on imaginary monsters as possible within a set time period.

Books to Share

Bennett, Gay. *A Family in Sri Lanka.* Minneapolis: Lerner, 1985. Depicts life in a small Sri Lankan village.

Wettasinghe, Sybil. *The Umbrella Thief.* New York: Kane/Miller, 1987. When each of the umbrellas he brought to the village disappears, Kiri Mama devises a plan to catch the thief. By one of Sri Lanka's favorite authors.

Chapter 15

Pakistan

When an ant's death is near, it sprouts wings.

◎◎

Pakistan declared its freedom from Great Britain and had its birth, in 1947, as a country proud of its Muslim heritage. More recently, in 1988, Benazir Bhutto became the first woman to lead a modern Islamic nation. Today, stories of the Prophet Muhammad and of his followers, as well as many folktales, help people to follow traditional values of simplicity, faith, and charity.

The Brass Cup

Once in Pakistan, a farmer and his wife were very hungry. For a whole year, the rains did not come and their crops did not grow. Both grew weak, waiting for clouds, hoping for rain.

"Today I'll search for roots to eat," said the farmer when he left one morning. He walked and walked into the forest, but found no food. After a long day, though, he came to the cave of a wise man who lived alone.

"My son," said the kind man. "You look tired. Rest and have some rice." The farmer eagerly ate the rice but then began to cry.

"Why do your tears come?" asked the wise man.

"Although I thank you, sir, for your great kindness," replied the farmer, "I cry when I think of my wife, starving at home while she waits for me." Hearing those sad words, the wise man went into his cave and came out carrying a brass cup.

"Take this," he said. "Whenever you wish to eat, hold it, and think of your favorite food." With many bows, the farmer thanked him and ran home. On the way, he stopped to try it out.

"How I would love to eat some flavored rice and chicken," he said. Suddenly, there it was before him, smelling quite delicious. He ate and ate and ate, unable to believe his good fortune. Then he hurried on. But again he stopped when he heard a mother's voice trying to comfort a hungry child.

"I'll find some food tomorrow, I promise. Now please go to sleep," begged the mother. The farmer, a good-hearted man, went up to her door.

"I can help you," he said, holding the cup and thinking of food. At once, fruits, nuts, rice and more appeared. With wide eyes, the child gobbled it all down. But the mother, a greedy woman, looked carefully at the cup. Later, while the farmer played with the child, the woman exchanged his cup for one of hers. Soon after, the farmer left and reached his home.

"Come, wife," he called eagerly. "Come see our new treasure."

She rushed out to greet him, looking for riches. But he held up only a rather tired looking brass cup.

"How silly you are, husband," she said. "That is only an old cup. Why do you make such a fuss?"

"No, it is more," he said and grinned. "Hold it and think of your favorite food." His wife slowly took the cup, wondering at his words. Her stomach cried so for food. She thought of rice, meat, yogurt. Soon her mouth watered, her teeth were ready to bite. But no food appeared. The cup just sat in her hand as she waited and waited.

"Husband, you are too cruel," she said at last. "Now I am even more hungry and we have nothing at all." Her husband took the cup, very puzzled. He wished for his favorite food. But still nothing happened. He shook his head, confused and sad. The two went to bed that night most unhappy. Early the next morning, he returned to the wise man's cave.

"Sir," he said, "your cup is no longer working. Please take it back."

"What do you mean?" replied the man, growing a little angry. "Of course the cup works. Are you lying to get another cup?"

"Oh, no, no," the farmer said. "And I thank you for your gift. I did get two good meals from it before it broke." Now the wise man knew that something was wrong.

"Tell me what you did after you left me yesterday," he said. When the farmer finished, the wise man understood. From his cave, he brought out a second brass cup.

"Give this to that woman," he instructed. "And she will get what she needs." The farmer nodded, thanked the man, and soon left. On he ran to the woman's house.

"Look," he said. "Yesterday I had my own cup with me. Today, I brought one for you. Hold it and enjoy it."

Very excited, she snatched the cup from him and held it tightly. But instead of fine food, two big sticks flew out and started to hit her. She cried and tried to hide, but the sticks chased her as she ran around and around the room.

"Stop them, stop them!" she screamed. "Here, take your cups back. Then stop the sticks!" She threw the cups to him and the sticks vanished at once into one cup. Satisfied, the man returned home.

"Now this cup will give food," he promised his wife. He gave her the right cup, and it worked perfectly.

Their home filled with fine tastes and smells as the two ate and ate. Then they invited their neighbors for a grand feast. After that, the kind farmer forgave the greedy woman, and shared food with her as well. But he did keep the cup with the sticks safely hidden, ready to use, just in case.

For Further Exploration of Pakistan

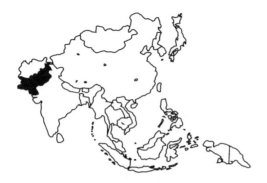

Pakistan, officially the Islamic Republic of Pakistan; South Asia
Area: 307,374 sq. miles
Population: 129,275,660 (1995 est.); 65% rural
Official language: Urdu, but only ten percent use it; Punjabi is spoken by a majority
Major city: Karachi

Activity: Rhyme

This lovely nursery rhyme is in Urdu, the national language of Pakistan. Its simple words are easy to say and fun to act out. Mime planting by bending over to plant, cutting with the swing of a knife, grinding with a stone rolling pin, cooking by stirring, and eating by using your fingers. The rhyme comes courtesy of the active, helpful Teachers' Resource Centre in Karachi, Pakistan.

Channa Kis Ney Boya?

Channa kis ney boya? kis ney boya? kis ney boya rey?
Channa hum ney boya, tum ney boya, sab ney boya rey.

Channa kis ney kata? kis ney kata? kis ney kata rey?
Channa hum ney kata, tum ney kata, sab ney kata rey.

Channa kis ney pisa? kis ney pisa? kis ney pisa rey?
Channa hum ney pisa, tum ney pisa, sab ney pisa rey.

Channa kis ney pakaya? kis ney pakaya?
*   kis ney pakaya rey?*

Channa hum ney pakaya, tum ney pakaya,
*   sab ney pakaya rey.*

Channa kis ney khaya? kis ney khaya? kis ney khaya rey?
Channa hum ney khaya, tum ney khaya, sab ney khaya rey.

English:

Who (kis) *planted* (boya) *the chick peas* (channa)?
We (hum) *planted it, you* (tum) *planted it, all of us* (sab)
*   planted it.*
Who cut it? (kata *means to cut*)
Who ground it? (pisa *means to grind*)
Who cooked it? (pakaya *is to cook, and is said quickly*)
Who ate it? (khaya *means to eat*)

Pronunciation hints: "Channa" as chun-na, "kis" as kiss, "pisa" as Lisa, "boya" as boe-ya, "ney" as nay, "pakaya" as puck-ayah, "khaya" as khah-yah, "hum" as hum, "tum" as toom, "sab" as sub.

Library/Information Skills Activity

As with many countries, the largest city in Pakistan is not the capital. Introduce children to another feature of the library's atlases, by pointing out that many maps use a special symbol, such as a star, to identify which city is the governmental center or capital. Have them identify which city is the capital of Pakistan, and then identify the capitals of other nations included in this book.

Books to Share

Khan, Eaniga. *Pakistan.* Chatham, NJ: Raintree/Steck-Vaughn, 1997. From the Country Insights Series.

Shepard, Allan. *The Gifts of Wali Dad.* New York: Macmillan, 1995. Wali Dad is an elderly grass cutter with simple tastes and a generous spirit.

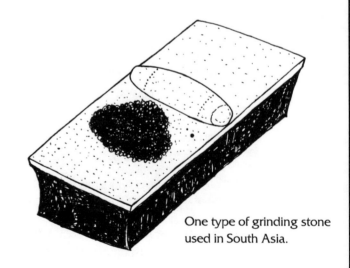

One type of grinding stone used in South Asia.

Chapter 16

China

A book is like a garden carried in the pocket.

෫෫෫෫෫෫෫෫෫෫෫෫෫෫෫෫෫෫෫෫෫෫෫෫෫෫෫෫෫෫

There are numbers of Chinese living in various lands and nations in Asia. And although there are political differences and resentments found, there is among many a pride in being Chinese, with an illustrious history, rich in art and story. The tales of Lazy Dragon, a thief much like Robin Hood, were told by Chinese storytellers centuries ago. When you tell this tale, do stop in the story before Lazy Dragon makes his plan and ask children what he could do. Older children sometimes guess his actual plan, while younger ones have all kinds of interesting suggestions.

Lazy Dragon

One evening, Lazy Dragon was walking down the road at twilight and met a gambling friend of his. The friend had just won a bag of gold, and he showed it proudly to Lazy Dragon.

"Lazy Dragon," said the gambler. "Since you're my friend, I know that you wouldn't steal my gold. But I believe that you couldn't steal it from me tonight!"

"Let us see," said Lazy Dragon with a grin. "If I can, you must buy me a fine meal tomorrow." His friend agreed and returned to his home. He told his wife what he had done.

"I'll help you watch the gold, husband," she said. "But first I'll cook a chicken to celebrate our good luck." She prepared the chicken and they ate half of it. Carefully, she went outside to put the rest in the kitchen shed, which was right next to a big well. When she returned, the two sat down, ready to stay up for hours, with the gold safely placed between them.

Lazy Dragon came to the house later that night and saw the couple still wide awake. He looked around at the kitchen out back and the well next to it. He knew that the house was locked tightly from inside, and that it had no chimney. Suddenly he had a plan. Can you guess what he did?

(Pause for ideas and continue when ready.)

He ran to the kitchen and made the sounds of a cat eating chicken.

"Oh, no," cried the gambler's wife. "It's a darn cat after the chicken. You watch the gold, I'll go chase him away." And out she ran. Lazy Dragon then moved to the well and dropped a large stone into it.

"Oh, no," cried the gambler when he heard the splash. "It's my darn wife. She fell down the well chasing the darn cat. I'll have to go get her." And he rushed out of the house, leaving the door open, the gold unguarded.

Lazy Dragon crept in, took the gold, then walked out. The next day, he knocked on their door.

"Here's your gold," he said with a smile. "And I feel very hungry." So the two friends went to have a grand meal paid for by the gambler. They had a good time laughing and telling tales. Late that night, the gambler returned home a little poorer and a little wiser, while Lazy Dragon went out to have another adventure.

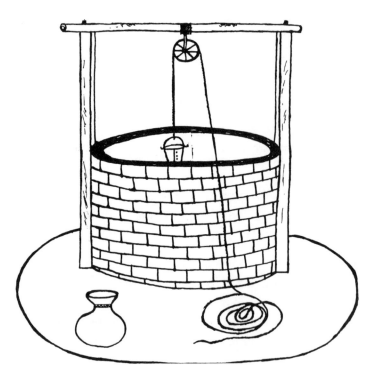

One type of Asian well.

For Further Exploration of China

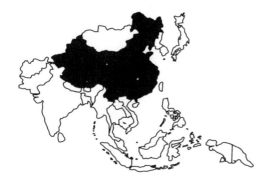

China, officially known as the People's Republic of China; East Asia
Area: 3,695,000 sq. miles
Population: 1,210,004,956 (1996 est.); 75% rural
Official language: Chinese
Largest city: Shanghai

Activity: Lantern Riddles

After challenging listeners' with "Lazy Dragon," you might all enjoy some Chinese riddles in a Riddle Lantern.

In the past, Chinese scholars often had Riddle Lanterns, where riddles were placed on three sides of a lantern, leaving the fourth translucent for light. The lanterns were hung near the scholars' doors for people to read and puzzle over. Prizes were given to those who solved them.

To make Riddle Lanterns

Make a big class lantern from a large box or make individual ones from smaller boxes (eg. ½ gallon milk cartons or Saltine cracker boxes). Children can glue pieces of bright, fluorescent paper on one side for a lantern glow.

Bits of colorful tissue paper can then be pasted onto decorate sides and top. Finally, put some of the following Chinese riddles on the sides, and attach a string or paper strip across the top to hold the Riddle Lantern.

Riddles

Two white walls and between them a yellow beauty. *(egg)*

Washing makes it dirty. When the wind blows, it wrinkles its skin. *(water)*

When I go out, I am thick and fat. When I come home, I am skinny like a skeleton. Then I am put in a corner and my tears flow. *(umbrella)*

Green bamboo are connected together and fly over high mountains. Great winds do not frighten them, but they fear fine rain. *(kite)*

Originally there are ten. Add ten more and there are still ten. *(gloves)*

Two pieces of bamboo drive white ducks through a narrow door. *(eating rice with chopsticks)*

A clever builder makes a white house without bricks that later becomes cloth. *(silk worm)*

It can't fly even though it seems to have wings. It travels far with no legs. *(fish)*

Green skin with white tummy; when cut open, it's all hollow. *(bamboo)*

Library/Information Skills Activity

Riddles are popular with kids throughout the world, and you can provide further enjoyment by introducing your children to these riddle sites on the Web:

Riddles
<http://www.kidsandcomputers.com/nicole/riddles.htm>

BBIT Riddles <http://www.abbit.com/riddles.html>

Books to Share

Hong, Lily Toy. *How the Ox Star Fell from Heaven.* New York: Albert Whitman, 1991. A Chinese folktale which explains how oxen came to be beasts of burden.

Waters, Kate. *Lion Dancer: Ernie Wan's Chinese New Year.* New York: Scholastic, 1990. Family and community celebrations of the Chinese New Year are detailed.

Wyndham, Robert. *Chinese Mother Goose Rhymes.* Cleveland: World Publishing, 1968. Another popular book on wordplay for children.

Yen, Clara. *Why the Rat Comes First: A Story of the Chinese Zodiac.* San Francisco: Children's Book Press, 1991. The Jade King invites the earth's animals for a feast, and decides to name a year after each of the twelve animals that attend.

Young, Ed. *High on a Hill.* New York: Collins, 1980. A popular picture book of Chinese riddles by an award-winning artist.

Chapter 17

Malaysia

*He that can see a louse as far away as China
is unconscious of an elephant on his nose.*

◎◎

In Malaysia, many languages, religions, and cultures co-exist, usually in peace. The landscape varies as well from sophisticated cities to quiet coastal villages and rich rain forests. Here is a tale from one of those forests on Sarawak, part of the Malaysian Federation.

In the Forest

Once in Sarawak, six girls went to gather wild roots in the forest. After a while, they were tired and started hungrily toward home. As they walked through the woods, they saw a warm light coming from a small house. Gayah, the most clever of the girls, was suddenly a little afraid.

"Let us get quickly away from here," she said. "I don't think this is a good place."

"Oh, you worry too much," said another girl. "And right now I'm hungry, so I'm going to stop there." She walked to the house, with the others following. At once, an old woman opened the door.

"Come in," she said. "You all look weary. Do rest here and eat." Gayah didn't trust the woman. She didn't want to eat her food. So she thought of a plan.

"Dear grandmother," she said. "We would love to eat. But first, please bring us some fresh water to drink."

"I will go get some at once," said the woman.

"When she goes for the water, we can leave," thought Gayah. But just then, the old woman waved a stick at the girls. Their heads nodded, very weary all of a sudden. Their arms and legs, too, felt so weak. The girls sank down on a mat as the woman quickly tied a big rope around them.

"Yes, some water would be wonderful to sip as I munch on your tasty bones," the woman screeched, opening her mouth to show her ***huge*** teeth. "I'll be back soon. Don't go away. I'll hold on to the rope just to make sure that you don't move." She ran down to the river, then tugged at her end of the rope.

"Good," she said. "They're still there." She filled her pot with water and gave the rope another tug.

"I can still feel them," she thought as she started back. Minutes later, she tried one last tug. "They haven't moved," she said hungrily and happily to herself.

But the girls had moved. Clever Gayah had carefully removed the rope and tied it around a big tree. Then the six had run and run into the forest. When the monster returned with the water, they were all gone.

"Ahaaaaa!" she cried. "Foolish girls! I'll get them." And she waved her stick, crying, *"Make a river with a hungry crocodile to stop those girls."* All of a sudden, a river appeared right in front of the six running girls. They almost fell into the wide open mouth of a huge crocodile there.

"Brother crocodile," said Gayah. "Please take us safely across this river."

"I'm starving," he said. "What will you give me to eat?"

"There are six of us," replied Gayah. "Carry five across and you can eat the sixth one!" The crocodile agreed and the first girl climbed on his back. She made it safely over and he came back for the next. After the second girl crossed, he carried the third, and the fourth. Then the fifth girl started over on his back. Quietly, Gayah, the sixth girl, jumped into the water and held on to his tail.

The crocodile left the fifth girl on land, and Gayah crept ashore as well. Then the crocodile swam back, thinking eagerly, "Now I get to eat the sixth one. And there she is." For he saw someone waving her arms madly on the shore. Of course, it was that evil creature who had just arrived.

"Take me across," she ordered as she jumped on his back. He swam to the middle of the river. But there, he slowed a bit and bounced her high up in the air. Then she dropped down right into his big mouth.

"Too bony," he thought. "Not very tasty at all." But he swallowed her anyway. So that was the end of that terrible creature.

Meanwhile, the girls finally reached their village. They told everyone of their adventure then enjoyed the safety of home. And after that, they were much more careful whenever they entered those woods.

For Further Exploration of Malaysia

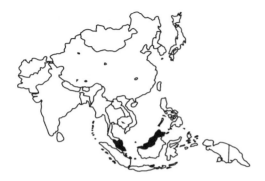

Malaysia; Southeast Asia
Area: 127,320 sq. miles
Population: 19,962,893 (1996 est.); 53% rural
Official language: Bahasa Malaysia
Largest city: Kuala Lumpur

Activity: Song

This is a children's song, *Tepok Amai-amai,* sung in kindergarten or first grade in Malaysia, and remembered by Jerry Teik-Chuan Lim. The different insects refer to the three main groups in Malaysia: the original Malay settlers, the Chinese, and the Indians. The tender coconut milk offered here is just one of the many gifts from this valuable tree. From it also come materials for cooking, construction, and for making coir, crafts, and toys. The words mean:

Clap little lady-bugs, grasshoppers, and colorful
  butterflies.
Clap, everyone.
Mother will give you coconut milk, rich and sweet,
the sweetest coconut milk from the young fruits.
Little brother, don't cry.
Mother has work to do.

Pronunciation hints: "k" is silent at end of word; "e" and "a" as in far; "i" as in meet, "o" as in go, "u" as in boo.

Library/Information Skills Activity

Have students practice using media center resources to solve problems. Propose a trip to Malaysia for the class. What kinds of things would the class want to know in order to pack for this trip? How far would they be travelling? How might they get there? What would they be eating? Sources might include the World Almanac, the atlas and globe, the web sites for travel and country information, encyclopedias and any books the library has on other countries.

To glimpse the largest Malaysian state, Sarawak, try: <http:www.isarawak,com.my/>

For some tasty Malaysian recipes, visit: <http://ucsee.eecs.berkeley.edu/~soh/recipe.html>

Books to Share

Day, Noreha Yussof. *Kancil and the Crocodiles.* New York: Simon & Schuster, 1996. The trickster mouse deer, Kancil, gets the greedy crocodiles to help him find the delicious rambutan fruit. One of the very few picture books about Malaysia.

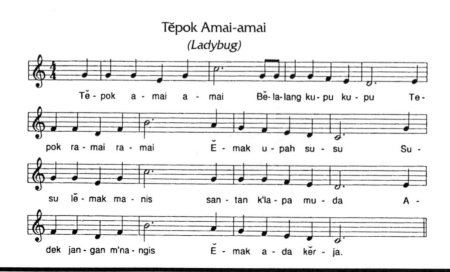

Tĕpok Amai-amai
(Ladybug)

Chapter 18

Korea

Though small, pepper is hot.

Today in Korea, students work very hard, using afterschool programs and even "English lessons over the telephone" to get ahead. Preparing for the competitive and crucial exam at the end of high school can take over a whole family's life for a year. In the past, the *kwago*, an important national exam, was used to choose civil servants. Stories, like this one, encourage the hard work and enterprising spirit needed to succeed in both tests and life.

Grain of Millet

Long ago, a young man journeyed to Seoul to take the national exam. With him, he carried a tiny grain of millet. Although it looked small, he knew that it might be of use.

After a day's journey, he came to an inn.
He gave the little grain to the innkeeper, saying,
"Guard this. It's my treasure."

But in the morning, the innkeeper ran up and said,
"Forgive me, but a rat has eaten your grain of millet."

"Then I'll take the rat," said the man.
So he took the rat
that ate the grain of millet.

He walked and walked that day and at night stopped again at an inn.
Giving the rat to the innkeeper, he said,
"Watch this. It's my treasure."

But in the morning, the unhappy innkeeper told him,
"Forgive me, but my cat killed your rat."

"Then I'll take the cat," said the man.
So he took the cat
that killed the rat
that ate the grain of millet.

He walked and walked and walked that day, too. At night, he stopped again at an inn. As he gave the cat to the innkeeper, he said, "Watch this well. It's my fortune."

But in the morning, the innkeeper said with a frown,
"Forgive me, but my horse stepped on your cat."

"Then I'll take the horse," the man replied.
So he took the horse
that stepped on the cat
that killed the rat
that ate the grain of millet.

That night, after a long day's ride, he stopped at another inn. He gave the horse to the innkeeper, saying, "Take care. This is my treasure."

However, early the next day, the innkeeper reported sadly that his ox had hurt the horse.

"Then I'll take the ox," said the man.
So he took the ox
that hurt the horse
that stepped on the cat
that killed the rat
that ate the grain of millet.

After a long day's walk, he stayed in a room right near the great city. He gave his ox to the innkeeper there, saying, "Please keep him safe."

But as the sun crawled up the next day, the innkeeper ran to the man crying, "Forgive me, sir. My son just sold your ox to a nobleman in the city."

"Then take me to that nobleman," demanded the young man. The innkeeper rushed to the nobleman's house and told him of the problem. Curious, the nobleman called for the young man to come. So he went boldly into that rich house and said, "I want my ox back right now."

"But sir," said the nobleman. "We have already cooked and eaten it."

"Then give me the first person who tasted it," the young man demanded. And he told the tale of the millet, the rat, the cat, the horse, and the ox. The nobleman was most impressed with the good fortune and the good mind of the young man.

"My friend," he said at last. "My daughter was the first to eat your ox. Since we are seeking a bridegroom for her and you seem quite right, perhaps this was meant to be."

Soon after, the two young people were happily married. Next, the husband passed the exam with highest marks, bringing more honor to his new home. So from then on, he and his family lived in great good fortune. And just think, it all started with one tiny grain of millet.

For Further Exploration of Korea

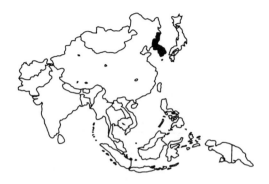

Korea, since 1948, divided into two parts: North Korea, known as the Democratic People's Republic of Korea; and South Korea, known as the Republic of Korea; Northeast Asia

Area: North Korea: 46,549 sq. miles; South Korea: 38,328 sq. miles

Population: North Korea: 23,904,124 (1996 est.) 64% urban; South Korea: 44,606,1995 (1995 est.) 84% urban.

Official language: Korean

Largest cities: P'yongyang (North Korea) Seoul (South Korea)

Activity: Lullaby

The repetition and wordplay in this story lend themselves nicely to simple songs. From Sunmi Pak, a teacher and mother, comes a lovely little lullaby, which is usually repeated softly several times. When Sunmi sings it, she pats her baby gently, in tim e to the steady, calming beat. Children can try patting imaginary babies or just tap their laps.

Ja jang, ja jang, ja jang, ja jang,
Woori aegi jaldo janda

Sleep, sleep, sleep, sleep
Our baby sleep well.

Library/Information Skills Activity

Many libraries now have multimedia encyclopedias that include music and video to accompany the text on a variety of topics. The example of the Korean lullaby in the previous activity should provide a good excuse to locate the article on Korea in your library's multimedia encyclopedia with your children. Have them locate some Korean music. Often the articles on different nations will include their national anthem or other native music.

Books to Share

McMahon, Patricia. *Chi-Hoon: A Korean Girl.* Honesdale, PA: Boyds Mill Press, 1993. A look at a young Korean student today.

Paek, Rohmer. *Aekyung's Dream.* San Francisco: Children's Book Press, 1988. A young Korean immigrant learns to adjust to her new life in America by heeding the words of an ancient Korean king.

Chapter 19

India

Patience is power.

In India, each region has its stories, legends, and local heroes. But great epics, like the story of Prince Rama in *Ramayana*, or the tale of the Pandava brothers in the *Mahabharata*, are known throughout the country. For centuries, stories from the Panchatantra collection have also taught children across India important values through small, enjoyable tales such as this.

Four Best Friends

Once in India, a crow, a mouse, and a turtle were the best of friends. The three met every day by the pond to talk and sing. They were always ready to help each other.

One day, while they sat together, a gold spotted deer ran up, her eyes huge with fear. In a frightened voice she cried, *"Help me. The hunters are coming to kill me."*

At once, Turtle pointed to some tall grass. Deer bent her head and slipped into the green. In seconds she was hidden. The three friends then moved around to cover her tracks. So when the hunters came, they glanced over but rode by without stopping.

"It is safe now," called Mouse after some time. Deer came out, thanked the three, and stayed to visit. She enjoyed herself and decided to live near her new friends.

Many days passed happily. Everything was peaceful, the forest smiled. Then one morning, Crow, Mouse, and Turtle met as usual. But their friend, Deer, did not come. They waited for hours and hours. When still she didn't come, they grew worried.

"We must go and search," said Crow and flew off at once. Suddenly, high flying Crow saw Deer below in a nearby clearing. Her leg was caught in a hunter's trap and she couldn't move. Crow quickly called his friends and they came to help.

"Don't worry, dear friend," said Turtle kindly. "We won't leave you. We'll help." As he talked and talked, comforting Deer, Mouse quickly nibbled through the rope and freed her.

Into the woods jumped Deer as Crow flew off and Mouse scampered away. But while slow moving Turtle crawled to safety, the hunter returned.

"My deer has escaped," he shouted furiously. "But at least I have a turtle." He picked up poor Turtle, tied a rope round his leg, and started toward home. Crow looked down as he flew and saw his poor friend being carried away. He quickly found Deer and Mouse.

"Now we must save Turtle," he cried. And they made a plan. Deer, with Mouse on her back, ran swiftly ahead of the hunter. Then she laid down in the path, as still as could be, while Mouse hid. Crow perched right on Deer's face, and looked like he was pecking at a dead body.

The hunter came up. He smiled when he saw the deer, thinking, "Ah, the deer didn't go too far. I'll just scare off that hungry crow and take my dinner home. It will be better than old turtle meat."

He tossed Turtle, took out his knife, and walked eagerly toward Deer. Meanwhile, Mouse ran right up and chewed off Turtle's rope. Turtle slipped into a nearby pond and Mouse scurried under a stone.

When the hunter was about three feet away, Deer suddenly jumped up and away to safety. At the same time, Crow flew off, leaving the hunter alone. He waved his hands and stomped his feet in a rage.

"Well, at least I have the turtle," he said after a while. He turned back but Turtle was gone. He looked all around, but never found him. The hunter was now alone in the silent forest. And very, very mad. But there wasn't anything he could do. So at last he walked home, with a frown on his face and nothing in his hands.

When his footsteps had faded and the woods were safe again, the four best friends met together at the pond. They had a grand time talking about their adventures while they celebrated both freedom and friendship.

For Further Exploration of India

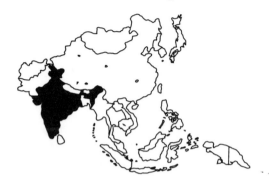

India, officially known as the Republic of India (or Baharat in Hindi); South Asia
Area: 1,222,243 sq. miles
Population: 952,107,694 (1996 est.); 73% rural
Official language: Hindi, with English as an associate language
Largest city: Mumbai (formerly Bombay)

Activity: Songs

A good friend and teacher, Shanta Gangolli, shared these two songs from western India, which are written as they should be pronounced.

Taa taa teengana
Yeden, yeden ahngana

This simple song, in Konkani language, is sung by mothers with their young children. Hands are held out in front of chest, rounded as if holding small balls. Then, keeping arms gently in place, hands alone make swinging motions, both hands moving in to center, then both hands twisting out in opposite directions, then continuing in and out in a gentle rocking rhythm. The notes, too, have that same rhythm, with soft slides from one to another. The first line is just wordplay, the second line means "such a small yard."

The next song, in Marathi language, is chanted, with actions:

Verse

1. *Ye-reh ye-reh pavsa* Come, come, rain

2. *Tula dayto pie-sa* I'll give you paisa (money)

3. *Pie-sa zala khota* The money was fake

4. *Pavoos ala mohta* But the rain came in torrents.

Actions

1. Look up to sky, use both hands, palms up, to call rain.

2. Right hand pretends to pick money from left open palm and offer it up to rain.

3. Look very sadly at empty palms, then turn hands over to show they're empty.

4. Both hands keep waving downward to mime a heavy rain.

Library/Information Skills Activity

India is one of the largest nations in the world in terms of its population. Ask your children which books they could use in the library to locate the name of the most populated nation in the world. Encourage them to select sources other than the encyclopedia.

Books to Share

Bond, Ruskin. *Cherry Tree.* Honesdale, PA: Boyds Mills Press, 1996. The gentle story of a girl in northern India who grows a cherry tree from seed.

Claire, Elizabeth. *The Little Brown Jay: A Tale from India.* Greenvale, NY: Mondo, 1995. A magical brown jay helps the Princess Maya and is rewarded in an unexpected way.

Demi. *One Grain of Rice: A Mathematical Folktale.* New York: Scholastic Press, 1997. A clever girl outsmarts a selfish rajah and saves her village.

Wolf, Gita. *Mala: A Woman's Folktale.* New York: Annick Press, 1996. A young girl tracks down the demon who swallowed the rain seed, and saves her village from drought.

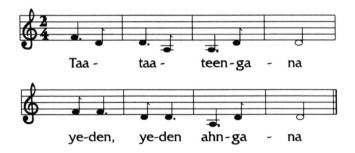

Taa - taa - teen-ga - na

ye-den, ye-den ahn-ga - na

Chapter 20

Japan

*Duty to parents is higher than the mountain,
deeper than the sea.*

Japanese storytellers love ghost stories as much as tellers around the world do. In the sophisticated theatrical style of *rakugo*, ghost stories are sometimes told in the summer to cool people off with a good chill! The shrine in this story is a Shinto shrine, which has several *torii* gates to walk under as you enter.

The Bet

Once long ago in the cold north of Japan, two men played a game. They sat near a lonely shrine which some people believed was haunted. As the two moved their pieces on the board, one man said, "Let us make a little penalty for this game. Whoever loses must go into the shrine at midnight tonight, all by himself."

His friend, Toshio, unhappily agreed for he was not very brave. So he played as best he could while the moon stared down. He played as long as he could while the clouds came to watch. But at last, he lost. Toshio looked at the dark shrine, then at his friend.

"Go into the shrine right now," the friend said. "You agreed."

"I don't want to go," said Toshio. "But I guess I must try." Somehow, from somewhere, he found the strength to move his legs. He walked slowly until he came to the outermost gate of the shrine.

"*Caaaarrrrrryyyy mmmeeeee, caaaaarrrrrryyyy mmeeeeee,*" sobbed a voice from deep inside the shrine. Toshio stopped, very scared.

"Whose voice is that?" he thought as his teeth chattered. He wanted to run right home, but he remembered his promise and forced his feet to walk under the first gate and down the path.

"*Caaarryyyyyy meeeee, cccaaaarrryy mee,*" sounded the voice, closer and louder as Toshio came to the second gate. Again he stopped. Again he wished to run and run far away. But he made himself go on, very slowly. He walked under the second gate and down the path to the shrine.

"*Ccaaaarrrry mmeeee, ccaarrryy mmmeeeee,*" cried the voice. It was very, very loud now. It came from the top of the tall tree right near the shrine. Tosio stopped. He closed his eyes, trying to be brave.

Shaking all over, he finally stumbled under the third gate and stopped. "Maybe it isn't a ghost," he thought to himself. "Someone could be caught in the tree. Maybe I can help." He made himself walk very slowly up to the tree.

"Caaaarryyyyy Meee, Caaarryy Meee," shouted the voice right above him now.

"All right, get on my back," Toshio whispered, waiting in dread. But there was no answer, no sound.

"Get on before I run away," he said a little louder. Nothing happened until *suddenly something very, very big jumped on his back.*

"Aaaahhhhhhhhhhhh!" He screamed, then ran and ran and ran all the way to his house. The **something** was still on his back. Quickly, he pushed open his door and then tried to shake it off.

"Please get down," he begged. But the thing only held on more tightly in the dark room. Toshio stumbled over to his bed on the floor and pleaded weakly, "Get off, I beg you." But it still held on. At last, Toshio collapsed right on his futon—so, so tired and weak from fright. Just then, he felt the thing leave his back.

He heard a sound in the corner, as if some thing had landed over there. But he didn't want to see what it was. Trembling, with his eyes closed in fright, the man buried his head under the quilt. He tried to forget his horrible night, and somehow, at last, he fell asleep.

Early the next morning, he woke while it was still dark. He tiptoed out of the room, still afraid of the thing in the corner. His wife was making tea. He spoke to her.

"Don't go inside that room," he said. "There is something terrible there." And he told her about his long walk to the shrine.

"But husband," she said. "You were brave and kind to carry that thing. He wouldn't hurt you now." The husband thought about her words for a moment. Then he shook his head and went to work, warning her one more time, just in case.

"Well," thought the wife. "I think he just had a nightmare. I'm sure there's nothing there. But perhaps I should check."

She picked up her broom and walked slowly inside. She crept closer and closer to the corner. There was no sound, and she couldn't see anything big and scary. In the soft daylight, there was no sign of a ghostly guest.

But suddenly she saw something glowing gently. She looked again. And she saw coins, spread out and shining right there on the floor. Gold coins that the visitor left for them. Gold coins left in thanks for Toshio's help.

For Further Exploration of Japan

Japan, also known as Nippon (origin of the sun);
East Asia
Area: 145,826, sq. miles
Population: 125,449,703 (1996 est.); 78% urban
Official language: Japanese
Largest city: Tokyo

Activity: A Drawing Song

Japan is a treasurehouse of both ghostly tales and children's songs. Various songs are enjoyed either by themselves or to accompany clapping or circle games, fingerplays, beanbag tossing, or other play.

One fascinating song type features drawings—of animals, numbers, and figures—made while words are sung. In this one, the words mean, roughly, *Little Roku* (roku also means 6) *eating a bean, became a bunny with long, long ears.* If needed, use pronunciation hints under "Two Tengu."

Library /Information Skills Activity

Encourage children to use a dictionary to help them understand words they might not know when reading on their own, for school or for pleasure. Words you might use from this story include shrine, haunted, and penalty, depending on the age of the children.

Books to Share

Look for translated picture books by these fine Japanese authors, so you can share the stories that Japanese children are also hearing and reading: Anno Matsumasa, Gomi Taro, Matsutani Miyoko, Matsuoka Kyoko, Miyazawa Kenji, Tejima Keizaburo, Ishii Momoko, Tsutsui Yoriko.

Two other highly recommended books for children are:

Friedman, Ina. *How My Parents Learned to Eat.* New York, Houghton, Mifflin, 1984. This is a delightful tale of the cultural differences between a Japanese girl and an American sailor.

Hamanaka, Sheila. *The Journey.* New York: Orchard, 1990. This nonfiction book uses vivid images from a mural by the author to relate the story of a tragic chapter in American history.

Additional Resources

Further Reading

Bielke, Patricia F. and Frank J. Sciara. *Selecting Materials for and about Hispanic and East Asian Children and Young People*. North Haven, CT: Shoe String Press, 1986.

Carrison, Muriel Paskin. *Cambodian Folk Stories*. Rutland, VT: Charles E. Tuttle, 1987.

Chin, Yin-lien, Yetta Center, Mildred Ross. *Traditional Chinese Folktales*. Armonk, NY: M.E. Sharpe, 1989.

Das, Surya. *The Snow Lion's Turquoise Mane: Tibetan Tales*. San Francisco: HarperCollins, 1992.

Dorson, Richard, ed. *Folk Tales of the World Series*. Bloomington: Indiana University Press. Includes several fine volumes on individual Asian countries.

Gomi, Taro. *An Illustrated Dictionary of Japanese Onomatopoeic Expressions*. Tokyo: Japan Times, 1989.

Hitam, Zakaria bin. *Folk Tales of Malaysia*. New Delhi: Sterling, 1986.

Jenkins, Esther C. and Mary C. Austin. *Literature for Children about Asians and Asian Americans: Analysis and Annotated Bibliography, with Additional Readings for Adults*. Westport, CT: Greenwood Press, 1987.

Kaignavongsa, Xay and Hugh Fincher. *Legends of the Lao*. Bangkok: Geodata System, 1993.

Khorana, Meena. *The Indian Subcontinent in Literature for Children and Young Adults: An Annotated Bibliography of English Language Books*. Westport, CT: Greenwood Press, 1991.

Kruse, Ginny Moore, and Kathleen T. Horning. *Multicultural Literature for Children and Young Adults*. Madison, WI: Cooperative Children's Book Center.

Lindgren, Merri V. ed. *The Multicolored Mirror: Cultural Substance in Literature for Children and Young Adults*. Ft. Atkinson, WI: Highsmith Press, 1991.

MacDonald, Margaret Read, ed. *The Folklore of World Holidays*. Detroit: Gale, 1992.

———. *Celebrate the World*. Bronx, NY: Wilson, 1994.

Mahmud, Sayyid Fayyaz. *There Was Once a King: Folktales of Pakistan*. Islamabad: Lok Virsa, 1981.

Mair, Victor H. *Painting and Performance*. Honolulu: University of Hawaii Press, 1988.

Manna, Anthony and Carolyn Brodie, eds. *Many Faces, Many Voices: Multicultural Literary Experiences for Youth*. Ft. Atkinson, WI: Highsmith Press, 1992.

———. *Art & Story: The Role of Illustration in Multicultural Literature for Youth*. Ft. Atkinson, WI: Highsmith Press, 1997.

Mayer, Fanny Hagin, ed. *Ancient Tales in Modern Japan*. Bloomington: Indiana University Press, 1984.

McDermott, Mustafa Yusuf. *Muslim Nursery Rhymes*. Leicester, U.K.: Islamic Foundation, 1981.

MultiCultural Review. Westport, CT: Greenwood. A quarterly journal devoted to a better understanding of ethnic, racial and religious diversity. Features articles and reviews.

Pellowski, Anne. *The World of Storytelling*. Bronx, NY: Wilson, 1990.

Ramanujan, A. K. ed. *Folktales from India*. New York: Pantheon, 1991.

Ryder, Arthur, trans. *The Panchatantra*. Chicago: University of Chicago Press, 1964.

Terada, Alice M. *The Magic Crocodile and Other Folktales from Indonesia*. Honolulu: University of Hawaii Press, 1994.

Thong, Le-Tinh. *Popular Stories from Vietnam*. San Diego: Institute for Cultural Pluralism, undated.

Vaidya, Karunakar. *Folk Tales of Nepal*. Kathmandu: Ratna Pustak Bhandar, 1979.

Vang, Lue and Judy Lewis. *Grandmother's Path, Grandfather's Way: Hmong Preservation Project*. San Francisco: Zellerbach Family Fund, 1984.

Viesti, Joseph and Diane Hall. *Celebrate! in South Asia*. New York: Lothrop, Lee, and Shepard, 1996.

———. *Celebrate! in Southeast Asia*. New York: Lothrop, Lee, and Shepard, 1996.

Winchester, Faith. *Asian Holidays*. San Francisco: Children's Press, 1996.

World Folklore Series from Libraries Unlimited, Englewood, Colorado. Excellent series with volumes of stories and cultural material from Thailand, Nepal, South India, and other parts of Asia.

Zong In-sob. *Folk Tales from Korea*. Elizabeth, NJ: Hollym, 1982.

Resource Centers: On & Off Line

Amica International
1201 1st Avenue South, Ste. 203
Seattle, WA 98134
Ph: 206/467-1035
Fax: 206/467-1522
E-mail: AMICA@ix.netcom.com
URL: http://www.islamicpublishers.com
Books, cards, children's magazine, Muslim world calendar

Asia for Kids
P.O.Box 9096
Cincinnati, OH 45209-0096
Ph: 800/765-5885
Fax: 513/271-8856
Asian books, toys, crafts

Asia Society
725 Park Ave.
New York, NY 10021
AskAsia Ph: 888/ASK-ASIA
AskAsia Fax: 888/FAX-ASIA
URL: http://www.askasia.org
Asian educational resource center

Brigham Young University
D.M.Kennedy Center for International Studies
Publication Services
280 HRCB
Provo, UT 84602
Publishes Culturgrams: concise, useful country notes

Cellar Book Shop
18090 Wyoming
Detroit, MI 48221
Books on and from Southeast Asia

Heritage Key
6102 East Mescal St.
Scottsdale, AZ 85254-5419
Ph: 602/483-3313
Fax: 602/483-9666
Asian books, dolls, games

KAZI Publications
3023-27 West Belmont Ave.
Chicago, IL 60618
Ph: 773/267-7001
Fax: 773/267-7002
E-mail: Kazibooks@kazi.org
URL: http://www.kazi.org
Materials on Islam and the Muslim world

Shen's Books and Supplies
8625 Hubbard Rd.
Arcadia, CA 95602-7815
Ph: 800/456-6660
Fax: 530/888-6763
E-mail:shensbooks@aol.com
URL: http://www.shens.com
Extensive multicultural catalog

South Asia Books
P.O. Box 502
Columbia, MO 65205
E-mail: sab@socketis.net
Books on and from South Asia

West Music
P.O. Box 5521
1208 5th St.
Coralville, IA 52241
Ph: 800/397-9378
Source of multicultural music and instruments

Selected Internet Sites

★ **Southeast Asia Web**
URL: http://www.gunung.com/seasiaweb
Well-organized site with many Southeast Asian links, including a great listing of sites on art and culture.

AccessAsia: Many web links organized by country and category. URL: http://www.accessasia.com

Material on **Aung San Suu Kyi** and the struggle to free Burma
URL: http://sunsite.unc.edu/freeburma/index.html

Asia-Pacific Magazine online
URL: http://coombs.anu.edu.au/asia-pacific-magazine

Bangkoknet: Many links to Southeast Asian sites.
http://www.bangkoknet.com/indochina/

Internet links dealing with **Greater China** (People's Republic of China, Tibet, Taiwan, Hong Kong, Macau, Singapore).
URL: http://www.univie.ac.at/Sinologie/netguide.htm

India Online: Resource links on India.
URL: http://indiaonline.com

Internet Guide to Buddhism and Buddhist Studies
URL: http://www.ciolek.com/WWWVL-Buddhism.html

The Islam Page: Resources about Islam
URL: http://www.islamworld.net/

Korea Web Weekly: Listings about Korea
URL: http://www.kimsoft.com/korea.htm

National Clearinghouse on U.S. – Japan Studies
URL: http://www.indiana.edu/~japan/

Newslink: Great way to find many Asian newspapers and journals
URL: http://www.newslink.org/nonusa.html

Pacific Bridge Arts: Links on Asian Arts
URL: http://www.pacific-bridge-arts.com/

Resources on **South Asian women**
URL:http://www.umiacs.umd.edu/users/sawweb/sawnet/news.html

Asian Art Treasures
http://sgwww.epfl.ch/BERGER/

Story Notes

All of the stories that appear in this book are traditional in their origin. They have been told for centuries, and have been revised and adapted by generations of storytellers and authors. The activities were drawn from the recommendations of friends and acquaintances, with their permission. Relatively few of these activities were ever previously published, and most were based on recollections of childhood games and crafts popular in the nations represented in this book.

The Two Tengu (p. 7)

With support from The Japan Foundation, I was able to meet over 200 Japanese storytellers as I traveled throughout Japan in 1991. I heard this tale then from various tellers, especially in the home libraries that are very popular in Japan. A variation of this story is also found in Florence Sakade's *Japanese Children's Favorite Stories*. (Rutland, VT: Charles E. Tuttle, 1958, 29–34); and retold by Karen Kawamoto McCoy in *A Tale of Two Tengu*. (Morton Grove, IL: Whitman, 1993)

Activity: The wordplays came from a good friend, storyteller Hosokawa Ritsuko of Noto peninsula, Japan.

The Kind Crow (p. 10)

Years ago, when doing a project on Southeast Asia for Wing Luke Asian Museum, Seattle, I heard bits of this tale at a meeting of consultants. I later found it also in Maung Htin Aung's *Folk Tales from Burma*. (New Delhi: Sterling, 1990, 32–35)

Activity: I found this game while browsing through musty back volumes of the *Indian Antiquary* in Madras University years ago. It was in the March 1894 issue, p. 84.

Judge Rabbit & Tiger (p. 13)

In 1983, I started a project, named *Singing Bamboo*, to collect stories from Southeast Asian refugees and then share them in local schools, museums, libraries, and over the radio as an introduction to Southeast Asian culture. The tales I most often heard from Cambodian refugees were about popular Judge Rabbit. This well-known story was collected from various women at Refugee Women's Alliance, Seattle, during a group story collecting time in 1985.

Activity: The song comes courtesy of Sam-ang Sam, Patricia Sheehan Campbell, and Judith Cook Tucker, who granted permission for me to use it in this book. It is found in the fine book by Campbell, Tucker, and Ellen McCollough-Brabson, *Roots and Branches: A Legacy of Multicultural Music for Children*. (Danbury: World Music Press, 1994, 22–25)

The Rich Sparrow (p. 16)

This tale was told during a storytelling workshop in Dhaka for the United States Information Agency (USIA). The teachers who shared it called it a children's favorite in Bangladesh. Slightly different versions are found in *Folk Tales of Bangladesh* by P.C. Roy Chaudhury (New Delhi: Sterling, 1990, 45–48), and *Folk Tales of Bangladesh* by Jasimuddin, translated by C. Painter and H. Jasimuddin. (Dacca: Oxford University Press, 1974, 76–84)

Activity: These two great rhymes come courtesy of Hasnain Sabih and his son Nayak, who publish a magazine for children in Bangladesh. We met years ago in Dhaka, and recently renewed our friendship over the Internet, through which they sent these two popular rhymes.

Kachba (p. 19)

Years ago I read this in Shankar's *Treasury of Indian Tales*. (New Delhi: Children's Book Trust, 1967, 17–24), and started to tell it, using a string puppet from Rajasthan state. Young children love the teasing chant, and the silliness of the princess.

Activity: Making kolams has been a favorite activity in our home for years. There are hundreds of traditional designs; Indian girls make their own books of favorites they see on the street, and so do we.

A Dog's Wish (p. 23)

During my *Singing Bamboo* collecting project, I heard this from Kham Pha, who was at that time an instructional aide in the Seattle Schools. The story is also found in *Folktales From Laos* by Somsy Vongsakdy (Seattle: Seattle Public Schools,1982, 58–61), with a slightly different ending: the buffalo wants to be the rope which ties him, then when he is a rope, a dog starts to gnaw him, and thus he returns to his original shape.

Activity: The idea came from a project my husband, Paramasivam, and I used with Southeast Asian children at a local international arts festival.

Juan & His Tricks (p. 26)

I pieced together this tale from talks with folklore scholar Dr. Kim Kyun Tae, who taught in the Philippines, and from *Philippine Folk Literature,* ed. by Damiana Eugenio. (Quezon City: University of Philippines, 1982)

Activity: These riddles come from a scholarly collection, Donn V. Hart's *Riddles in Filipino Folklore.* (Syracuse, NY: Syracuse University Press, 1964), and from *Laughing Together.* (Delhi: National Book Trust, 1991)

Watching the Garden (p. 29)

I adapted this from a tale I heard Thai teachers mention while on retreat at a southern Thai monastery, 1975. Another version of this story appears in Jenny Watson's *Favourite Stories from Thailand.* (Singapore: Heinemann Asia, 1976, 25–28). This chain type of tale is popular throughout the world; for two other related versions, see Anne Pellowski's *A World of Children's Stories.* (New York: Friendship Press, 1993, 23 and 161–163)

Activity: The basket weaving project comes from the Thai exhibit at the Seattle Children's Museum, and is used with their kind permission.

We Want Rice (p. 32)

When I was in Nepal in 1974, I had the good fortune to trek up around Annapurna. On that amazing trip, every night I stayed with a different Nepali family. Usually, communication was very limited due to language challenges, but on several nights I found someone who spoke English, and on such a night, I heard this tale.

Activity: My husband and I tried this activity in a Seattle preschool when our son was a student.

The Green Frog (p. 35)

While in Korea in 1996, I heard this very well-known tale in several storytelling classes and swap sessions. A version is also found in Suzanne Crowder Han's *Korean Folk and Fairy Tales.* (Elizabeth,NJ: Hollym, 1991, 32–33). In the very useful *Type Index of Korean Folktales* by Choi In-hak (Seoul: Myongji University, 1978, 3–40), he lists twelve variants of the tale collected and published in Korea. A recent picture book version is Yumi Heo's *The Green Frogs.* (Boston: Houghton Mifflin, 1996)

Activity: A dear friend and my first guide to Korean culture, Choi Yong Jin, helped me with this section.

A Stranger (p. 38)

In 1975, I heard this story from an Indonesian storyteller, who I knew only as Robbie. He had traveled throughout the islands, collecting ideas and tales, and settled near Peliatan, Bali.

Activity: I have made such books for several years. A good resource with related projects is *Contemporary Southeast Asian Arts and Crafts* by Thelma Newman. (New York: Crown, 1977)

Dinh Tien Hoang (p. 41)

When I was collecting stories from Southeast Asians, I met often with Emanuelle Chi Dang at Refugee Women's Alliance, Seattle. She was kind enough to share this tale during a conversation about Vietnamese heroes. A brief version is also found in *An Introduction to Vietnamese Literature,* by Maurice M. Durand and Nguyen Tran Huan. (New York: Columbia University Press, 1985, 43)

Activity: The game is courtesy of Cliff Sloane, who collected it in 1995, through the kindness of the teachers and students of the Vietnamese Language School of Minneapolis, directed by Thuthanh Nguyen.

The Corn & the Lazy Farmer (p. 44)

I heard this story from my friend, Blia Xiong, in 1984, for the *Singing Bamboo* project on Southeast Asian stories.

Activity: Over the years, I've made various storytelling props with young listeners. The story cloth is one of my favorites, not only because the children enjoy it, but also since models and books on the cloths are available in the U.S.

The Pond (p. 47)

This is one of my son Manu's favorite *Jataka* tales; he discovered a version in the classic comic series popular in India, *Amar Chitra Katha.* There are almost 550 *Jataka* tales relating the Buddha's past lifetimes, although not all are equally known. One often heard in Sri Lanka, but too long and difficult to relate here, is the tale of the generous Prince Vessantara, the last lifetime before the birth of the Buddha. A more elaborate version of "The Pond" can be found in E. B. Cowell's translation, *The Jataka,* Vol. 1. (London: Pali Text Society, 1973, 54–56)

Activity: While in Colombo, Sri Lanka, in 1992, I heard

some of these. Others I found in Nandasena Ratnapala's *Folklore of Sri Lanka*. (Colombo: State Printing Corporation, 1991), and in *Laughing Together*. (Delhi: National Book Trust, 1991)

The Brass Cup (p. 50)

After my program for USIA in Islamabad, 1992, an interesting group of Western and Pakistani folks sat and swapped tales, including this one.

Activity: This delightful song comes from the Teachers' Resource Centre in Karachi which is doing wonderful work training teachers and promoting education for all. Although I gave a workshop there in 1992, they sent this song to me after they discovered my web page and we got back in touch through the Internet. It is used with their permission.

Lazy Dragon (p. 53)

I have been telling Lazy Dragon tales ever since I discovered versions of them in *The Courtesan's Jewel Box*, by Yang Xianyi and Gladys Yang. (Beijing: Foreign Languages Press, 1981) The book contains a fascinating collection of stories told by Chinese storytellers in the tenth through the seventeenth centuries. As a folklore character, Lazy Dragon seems related to Robin Hood; as a skillful thief, he could be compared to "The Master Thief" from Germany, found in Jane Yolen's *Favorite Folktales from Around the World*. (New York: Pantheon, 1986, 138–144)

Activity: I gathered these riddles at the helpful Chinese Information and Service Center, Seattle, from Professor Jeff Tsay, who has taught me much about Twaiwan through our E-mail conversations.

In the Forest (p. 56)

Folktales from Malaysia are, unfortunately, hard to find. I have drawn this story from several traditional sources, but a variation appears in *Favourite Stories from Borneo*, by Leon Comber. (Kuala Lumpur: Heinemann Asia, 1975, 23–24)

Activity: This song comes from Jerry Teik-Chuan Lim,

used with the permission and courtesy of the publisher for Campbell et al, *Roots and Branches: A Legacy of Multicultural Music for Children*. (Danbury: World Music Press, 1994, 52-55)

Grain of Millet (p. 59)

In 1996, several Korean librarians told me this popular tale. It is also found in various story collections, including Han's *Korean Folk and Fairy Tales*. (Elizabeth, NJ: Hollym, 1991, 216–220), and Choi In-hak's *Type Index of Korean Folktales*, where he lists eight variants on pages 74–75. However, it is not usually written in this simpler, cumulative tale structure which young listeners and beginning readers enjoy.

Activity: The lullaby comes from my dear friend, Sunmi Pak, who sang it to her two children in Seattle.

Four Best Friends (p. 62)

This is a very well-known tale in India. I heard it from a longtime friend and educator, Indira Seshagiri Rao. Variations are found in several editions of the *Panchatantra* published by National Book Trust, India Book House, and other Indian publishers.

Activity: The two songs came from Shanta Gangolli, a good friend who kindly shared them with me.

The Bet (p. 65)

I heard this at an incredible storytellers' retreat in a hot springs inn nestled amongst the mountains of northern Japan in 1991. At the evening telling, Munakatasan, a storyteller from Aomori, gave us a slow, suspenseful version of this tale. In Yanagita Kunio's excellent *Guide to the Japanese Folk Tale* (edited by Fanny Hagin Mayer, Bloomington: Indiana University Press, 1986, 69), he lists ten versions of this story.

Activity: This drawing song is widely known in Japan, as are others like it. I heard it while a student at the Japanese Language School in Seattle, and later in Japan from storyteller Hosokawa Ritsuko of Noto, and from Inada Kazuko, a talented writer and folklore collector in Okayama.